Making the Sign of the Cross

Janet Hodgson has worked and written extensively in the area of mission. She developed the *Healthy Churches* resources with Robert Warren for Church House Publishing and before retirement worked as a missioner in the Diocese of Durham.

She is the author of The Faith We See (MPH) and lives in South Africa.

Making the Sign of the Cross

A creative resource for seasonal worship, retreats and quiet days

Janet Hodgson

CANTERBURY
PRESS
Norwich

First published in 2010 by the Canterbury Press Norwich
Editorial office
13–17 Long Lane,
London, EC1A 9PN, UK

Canterbury Press is an imprint of Hymns Ancient and Modern Ltd
(a registered charity)
St Mary's Works, St Mary's Plain,
Norwich, NR3 3BH, UK

www.scm-canterburypress.co.uk

British Library Cataloguing in Publication data

A catalogue record for this book is available
from the British Library

978 1 84825 006 2

Typeset by Regent Typesetting, London
Printed and bound in Great Britain by
CPI Antony Rowe, Chippenham SN14 6LH

For Jay

Family, and friends in McGregor

CONTENTS

Foreword   xi
Preface   xiii
List of Illustrations   xvii
Introduction   1

Part 1   Crosses Over the Ages and Around the World   9

  1 Background Information   13
      Early History of Crosses   13
      Inculturation of the Cross   14
      Handout 1: Basic Forms of Crosses and the Crucifix   15
      Handout 2: Orthodox Examples   19
      Bible Study or Reflection   20

  2 Images of the False Cross   21
      The Crusading and the Crucified Church – Introduction   21
      Handout 3: The Emperor Constantine   21
      Handout 4: Crosses of the Crusaders   22
      Handout 5: Columbus and the Conquistadores   23
      Modern Examples of the False Cross   25
      Images of the False Cross in Film   26

  3 True Images of the Cross   27
      Saints and Their Crosses   27
      Worship to Honour the Saints of God   27
      Handout 6: St Francis + Prayer   28
      Handout 7: St Dominic + Prayer   29
      Handout 8: St Andrew and St Peter   30
      Celtic Crosses   31
      Handout 9: Irish Solar and Standing Crosses   31

Handout 10: St Brigid's Cross + Prayer   34
Handout 11: St Cuthbert   36
Irish Penal Cross   37
Compostela, Maltese and Coventry Crosses   37
Handout 12: The Way of St James the Great to Santiago de
Compostela   37
The Maltese Cross   38
Coventry Cathedral Cross of Nails   39
Closing Prayers   40

Part 2   Living the Cross   **41**

4 Big Cross, Little Crosses   **43**
Programme for a Half-Day or Evening Session   43
Opening Worship   43
Handout 13: Big Cross, Little Crosses   44
Our Personal Little Crosses of Pain and Suffering   46
Bible Study No. 1   46

5 Good Friday Pilgrim Stories   **47**
Programme for a Half-Day Event   47
Good Friday Pilgrims   47
Handout 14: Being Transformed by a Crucifying Event   48
    Story no. 1: A French Roman Catholic Archbishop   48
    Story no. 2: Abraham Lieta, Anglican Priest in Lesotho   49
    Story no. 3: John, a Priest in England   49
Bible Study No. 2   49
Handout 15: The Cross as a Symbol of Non-Violent Resistance in
South Africa   50
    Story no. 4: Prophetic Witness of Clergy   50
    Story no. 5: Archbishop Tutu as the Rabble-Rouser for Peace 50
    Story no. 6: Good Friday in Durban: Peace through the Cross 51
    Story no. 7: The Young and the Old   51
Handout 16: Carrying the Cross for One's Community   52
    Story no. 8: Latin American Martyrs   52
    Story no. 9: Witnessing as a Persecuted Christian Minority in a
    Muslim Country   53
    Story no. 10: Prophetic Action by Filipino Women   53

Handout 17: Christian Witness in the Sudan   54
   Story no. 11: 'Forever Stuck to the Cross'   54
Things To Do Relating to Good Friday Pilgrims   56
Handout 18: Healing of the Crucified, Wounded Earth   57
   Story no. 12: A Compassionate Ministry in South Africa   57
   Story no. 13: Healing the Wounded Earth in Britain   58
Things To Do in Healing Our Earth   59
Closing Worship: Liturgy for the Dispossessed   59
Liturgies on Creation   61

Part 3   Working with Crosses   **63**

6 Workshops with Crosses   **65**
Programme for a Weekend Event   65
Opening Worship   65
Saturday Morning Programme (with options)   66
Handout 19: Introductory Talk on Crosses   67
Saturday Afternoon and Evening Programme   69
Closing Worship   71
Sunday Morning Programme   72
Handout 20: Additional Exercises with Crosses   74
   Exercise no. 1: Questions focusing on faith and mission   75
   Exercise no. 2: Making a visual mission statement with crosses 75
   Exercise no. 3: Exploring crosses in your church   76
   Exercise no. 4: The cross as a flower festival theme   76
   Exercise no. 5: Things to do with crosses   77
   Exercise no. 6: Bible study   77

7 The Way of the Cross   **79**
Programme for a Half-day Event   79
Opening Worship with Meditation   80
Handout 21: The Stations of the Cross   81
Doing Theology Through Art   82
Handout 22: Biblical References Relating to the Stations of the Cross   82
Dramatization of the Passion   84
A Good Friday Service Using Pictures of the Passion   85
Making Your Own Stations of the Cross   86
Handout 23: Suggestions for Making Your Own Stations   87

Handout 24: Additional Exercises   91
    Exercise no. 1: Discussion using films on the Passion   91
    Exercise no. 2: Discussion of Handel's interpretation of the
    Crucifixion   92

Part 4   Praying at the Foot of the Cross   93

  8 **Making the Sign of the Cross**   95
    Programmes – Full and Half Day or Evening   93
    Opening Worship   95
    Handout 25: Making the Sign of the Cross   95
    Reflection and/or Discussion   99

  9 **Prayer and Meditation**   100
    Worship and Reflection   100
    Handout 26: Prayer as Holy Silence   102
    Bible Study No. 3   103
    Handout 27: Prayer as Presence   104
    Topics for Discussion   105
    Handout 28: Worship and Talk on Meditation   105
    Handout 29: Praying with a Holding Cross   108
    Things To Do   110

 10 **Labyrinths, Prayer Stations and a Retreat on the Streets**   111
    Handout 30: Labyrinths – Prayer Stations – a Retreat on the Streets 111
    Walking a Labyrinth   111
    Prayer Stations   112
    A Retreat on the Streets   112
    Closing Prayer   113

Further Resources   114
    Further Reading, Prayers, Meditations   114
    Selection of Internet Sources   115
    Pictures of Crosses   116
    Hymns Relating to the Cross   117

FOREWORD

I first came to know Janet and her work when she was Adviser in Local Mission in the Diocese of Durham and I was Warden of Cranmer Hall. Janet's passion for mission and for Christ is infectious and compelling. I learned much from working with her. In particular Janet modelled for me that if people are to become excited by mission then they must first be excited and stirred and changed by the person of Christ. Over several years I invited her to come and work with ordinands in Cranmer Hall with her extensive collection of pictures and postcards of Jesus. The sessions were often very powerful and, for some, life changing. They were also sometimes uncomfortable and encouraged people to challenge authority and the way things were done in the name of Christ.

Janet has already had considerable influence on the Church in the United Kingdom and beyond through the Healthy Churches process and her creative partnership with Robert Warren. That process flowed from an original day conceived by Janet in the Diocese of Durham and has gone on to influence thousands of local congregations.

Janet is a person of considerable courage and great good humour. Her work uses pictures and crosses to help us see and articulate what we believe. It is simple, truthful and accessible without being simplistic. It always in my experience points to Christ and creates space for people to engage with one another and with the Lord who calls them.

I believe that the book you are holding in your hand has the potential to be a powerful tool in Christian formation of communities and individuals. By the grace of God and for the good of his Kingdom, use it well.

The Rt Revd Dr Steven Croft
Bishop of Sheffield

PREFACE

The material in this book has been tried and tested over many years in Britain and South Africa. It has been used with every imaginable size of group as well as with individuals, clergy and laity, ordinands and lay ministers, confirmation candidates and seekers, churchgoers and non-churchgoers of all ages and abilities, and in multicultural and ecumenical settings.

Their enthusiastic responses have inspired me to share something of my passion for working with crosses, whether this be on retreats or quiet days, in training or worship, in spiritual direction or as sermon material, in small fellowship groups, or parish workshops. This might be for an hour, evening, half a day, full day, or weekend. The options are never ending. All it requires is imagination as to how different aspects of the material can best be used, and whether this will be for a one-off event or a course lasting a few weeks.

When I first started this work, an unusual experience was seeing members of the Durham Bishop's Council share their faith for the first time ever through the medium of crosses: the diocesan bishop with his diocesan secretary, an archdeacon with a woman churchwarden, an area dean with the diocesan financial adviser. They discussed why some had chosen a plain cross and others a crucifix, touching deeply on their personal spirituality.

Recently, nothing could have been more mixed than a Lent group in McGregor, the village where I live, two hours away from Cape Town. In our group of 17, ages ranged from 25 to 81, half of whom were non-churchgoers. Our group included Anglicans, Roman Catholics, a German-speaking Lutheran, a French speaker from a Swiss mission family, two atheists (one now making a cross for her bedroom), a Dutch Reformed Church (Calvinist) minister, a DRC laywoman, and an Afrikaans-speaking young man from a charismatic house church. Only the limitations of my home limited our numbers: this in a small community.

As with my previous book, *The Faith We See: Working with Images of Christ* (Peterborough: Inspire, Methodist Publishing House, 2006), my hope would be that crosses might be used for personal faith development and theological reflection, spiritual enrichment and worship, meditation and prayer, and the living out of the gospel in a local context. Crosses are more tactile than images, but pictures are equally useful, and advice is given as to how to make a collection in both mediums.

Background information is given on different representations of the cross over time, together with many stories as to how both saints and ordinary people have tried to make the sign of the cross a living symbol in different parts of the world. This provides input for crosses to be used in a variety of events, or anywhere where believers come together to nourish their spirituality, as well as for private reflection, prayer and praise. My hope is that this material will appeal to a broad range of people, and that the many practical ideas will encourage them to witness boldly to Christ in the world around them.

I would like to express my sincere gratitude to all those who have encouraged me in this work over the years, supported me through the vicissitudes of writing, and supplied me with crosses from around the world. I now have a collection of over 300 crosses in all shapes, sizes and mediums, most on display in my study.

In England, I am deeply indebted to Michael Turnbull, former Bishop of Durham, Stephen Conway, now Bishop of Ramsdale but former Archdeacon of Durham, and Steven Croft, now Bishop of Sheffield but former Principal of Cranmer Theological College. Geoff Lowson, Priest in Charge of Tyneside, and Monica Lowson have been faithful friends through many years of this work.

In South Africa, I am deeply indebted to my family for their unfailing support; and to my sister, Gillian Lord, on the last leg of the journey. In McGregor, Yvonne Courtin has nourished me with food, while Francois Holmes has lit endless candles and prayed many prayers on my behalf. A special word of thanks to Corrie van der Colff, who has kept me going spiritually and physically through a Pilates programme, and given so much encouragement as a friend and mentor.

The Revd Robert Cooper, Elsabe van der Colff and Geoff Neil have all contributed photographs for which I am extremely grateful; and Ann Snaddon laboured long and hard over the illustrations of crosses. I am deeply indebted to Christine Smith, Publishing Editor with SCM-Canterbury Press, for her enthusiastic support and guidance. I would also like to thank Rebecca Hills for her work on the text and her imaginative use of illustrations, Joanne Hill for her meticulous proofreading, and Leigh Hurlock who created the cover.

Finally, I am very grateful for the friendship and wisdom of the Revd Jay S. Kothare, a retired Anglican priest in Manchester. In the writing of this book, I am deeply indebted to him for being an indispensable source of inspiration and for his overall theological input, more especially the worship.

Acknowledgements for permission to publish their material must be given to:

The Central Board of Finance of the Church of England 1980; The Archbishop's Council 1999 – Collect for Holy Cross Day, *The Alternative Service Book 1980*.

The Anglican Church in Aotearoa, New Zealand and Polynesia – two Collects for Holy Cross Day, *A New Zealand Prayer Book. He Karakia Mihinare o Aotearoa, 1988.*

The Revd Dr John de Gruchy for a meditation from *Cry Justice*, London: Collins, pp. 232–3.

Estate of the late John V. Taylor for a prayer from *A Matter of Life and Death*, London: SCM Press, 1986.

Angela Ashwin for the use of prayers in the leaflet accompanying the wooden Holding Crosses.

Fr Bart Espartero for two prayers, and USPG: Anglicans in World Mission, *Transmission*, Advent 1993.

Anonymous author of 'A Special Lenten Fast from South America' and CAFOD, in their *Prayer Pack*, Easter 2009.

Unknown author of a prayer from the Christian Conference of Asia.

Canon Morriat Gabula for prayers and correspondence, 2006 and 2009.

ILLUSTRATIONS

1 Boat and anchor (Ann Snaddon)   1
2 Chi Rho cross (Ann Snaddon)   3
3 St Cuthbert's and Canterbury crosses (Geoff Neil)   6
4 Traditional cross shapes (Elsabe van der Colff)   13
5 Latin cross (Ann Snaddon)   15
6 Greek cross (Ann Snaddon)   15
7 Ethiopian crosses (Elsabe van der Colff)   16
8 Traditional Swastika cross and right-facing decorative Hindu form
   (Ann Snaddon)   16
9 Tau cross (Ann Snaddon)   17
10 Jesus inside an Ankh (Geoff Neil)   17
11 St Andrew's cross (Ann Snaddon)   18
12 Traditional crucifix (Ann Snaddon)   18
13 The Eastern cross (Ann Snaddon)   19
14 The Crusaders' or Jerusalem cross (Ann Snaddon)   22
15 St George's cross and Red Cross (Ann Snaddon)   23
16 Arriving missionaries (USPG)   24
17 San Damiano cross (Elsabe van der Colff)   28
18 Two Dominican crosses (Ann Snaddon)   30
19 Sun cross (Ann Snaddon)   32
20 Early Celtic cross (Ann Snaddon)   32
21 Celtic cross (Ann Snaddon)   33
22 St Brigid's cross (Ann Snaddon)   35
23 St Cuthbert's cross (Ann Snaddon)   36
24 Irish penal cross (Geoff Neil)   37
25 St James the Great's cross (Ann Snaddon)   37
26 Cross of the Order of Santiago (Ann Snaddon)   38
27 Maltese cross (Ann Snaddon)   38
28 Coventry Cathedral cross (Robert Cooper)   39
29 Set of three crosses (Ann Snaddon)   44
30 Three African crosses (Elsabe van der Colff)   48

31 Peace cross (Ann Snaddon)   51
32 Barbed Wire Crucifix (Elsabe van der Colff)   52
33 Sudanese mud cross (Christian Aid)   54
34 Sea pinks and crosses (Robert Cooper)   58
35 Aids service (Robert Cooper)   63
36 South African child looking at a cross (source unknown – South Africa) 63
37 'Raped' (source unknown –South Africa/ on a cross alongside a road in
    Johannesburg)   63
38 Man lying on a broken cross (African artist unknown – South Africa) 78
39 11th Station from Bloemfontein church (Janet Hodgson)   83
40 Fenwick Lawson's *Pietà 2* (Robert Cooper)   84
41 Amnesty Candle, Salisbury Cathedral   87
42 Bishop's Confirmation (Robert Cooper)   96
43 Khotso House tapestry, Johannesburg (unknown)   101
44 *The Power and the Glory* by Coral Bernadine   101
45 'You have surrounded me with joy' (unknown artist, South Africa) 102
46 A holding cross (Ann Snaddon)   108
47 Holding crosses (Geoff Neil)   109

INTRODUCTION

At the Foot of the Cross

The cross is the ultimate symbol of God's unconditional and sacrificial love for all creation. 'For God so loved the world that he gave his only Son' (John 3.16); and again, 'No one has greater love than this, to lay down one's life for one's friends' (John 15.13). The New Testament Greek has a special word for this unique love of God – *agape*. This self-denying love is such a distinctive hallmark of the gospel that St Paul identifies it as 'the word of the cross' (1 Corinthians 1.18).

The cross is thus the most singular icon of the Christian faith. The problem is that we have allowed it to become sanitized and prettified, to be worn as a piece of jewellery devoid of any spiritual meaning. But there is no such thing as a 'nice' cross. In Jesus' time, the cross was a shameful instrument of torture and execution reserved for condemned criminals. No wonder the early Christians were reluctant to use it as a sign of their faith. Instead, they chose to disguise it as a trident, the mainmast of a ship or an anchor, symbolizing heavenly hope anchored to the cross of Christ.

1 – Boat and anchor

The cross is not an abstract theological concept but a stark historical reality. In our Creed we confess to our faith that 'Jesus was crucified for us under Pontius

Pilate'. The cross is the medium and the venue that God chose to bear our suffering in Christ. There is nothing we endure that Jesus has not endured on the cross. The crucified Saviour is ever present with us in all our trials and tribulations, large and small, and listens and responds to our prayers and supplications. The cross thus reflects our little crosses, the pain and suffering in our ordinary, individual lives, whatever they may be.

The cross also points to the suffering caused by human sin. This suffering is both personal and corporate. Corporate suffering becomes manifest as social bondage and political oppression perpetuating poverty, exploitation and wars. The crucified Jesus is present and alive as much in the collective lives of communities and nations as in the suffering in our private lives. Many, especially in the affluent West, are slow to acknowledge this dimension of the cross of Jesus, which exposes the role of human sin in the creation of suffering inflicted on humans, animals and the ecology. According to Archbishop Desmond Tutu, the Bible is the most subversive document in the world. A well-known poster has him saying: 'I am puzzled about which Bible people are reading when they suggest religion and politics don't mix.' Tutu fearlessly led his crucified people in the struggle against apartheid, not despite, but thanks to his Christian commitment.

When people in poor countries hear the story of Jesus, they experience it as their own story, as if he was being incarnated in their very midst. The good news of the crucified and risen Christ revives their faith in God, giving them hope and courage to face suffering and oppression, and to strive for justice. The cross warns us that it is not optional for Christians to seek the Kingdom and reminds us that God in Christ proactively intervened in the politics of compassion and peace. As believers, we must constantly ask ourselves whether we have chosen to gather under the cross or to walk away from it. The Church that gathers at the foot of the cross prays for the Kingdom, seeking to hallow the sinful structures of our divided world, and heal the wounds of the bruised people of God.

Historically, we in the West have prided ourselves on taking the Christian faith to every corner of the world. But, somehow, we seem to have lost the sense of the intensity, immediacy and relevance of the cross in the life of the Church at home. An engagement with the cross of Jesus is indispensable as an ongoing reality check which would ensure that our liturgy, prayer, mission, evangelism, theology and Christian witness are all credible in the eyes of the oppressed people of the world. We not only proclaim the cross but, as disciples of Christ, we share in its risk and pain.

Embracing the cross, we cannot be far from Jesus, for Jesus is where the cross is. Denying ourselves and taking up our crosses (cf. Matthew 16.24), we walk with Jesus through the whole wide world, preaching the gospel, incarnating the word of the cross through the endless shapes, symbols and forms of humanity's diverse cultures and traditions.

2 – Chi Rho cross

Pick-and-Mix Planning of Programmes

The book is divided into Parts 1–4 so as to encompass a broad spectrum of themes relating to the cross, with plentiful handouts. Different programmes offer options for different events, be they retreats, Quiet Days, parish away-days, courses, or seasonal worship. These could be an evening, a half or full day, a weekend or a couple of days on retreat. The material is well suited to prayer and meditation, with an abundance of stories to help make the cross a reality in our lives. In addition, provision is made for activities involving working with crosses, as well as Bible studies, worship and things to discuss and do. The CD-ROM offers a range of images of crosses. Some relate specifically to the text, while others can be used in meditation, prayer and worship.

The detailed Contents allows for a pick-and-mix approach. The selection of relevant material depends on the purpose of the event and the time available. Different modules are added as required. The programmes offer guidelines for timing, but this again is flexible. As to seasons, the cross is a natural focus during Lent and Passion Week, while Holy Cross Day on 14 September is another key date; but the material is not tied to any particular season and can be used throughout the year.

Part 1 focuses on background information about crosses over the ages. In addition to identifying the basic forms of crosses, we look at images of both the false cross over time, and the true cross of some of the saints. Part 2 is rich in stories of how people around the world have tried to live out the meaning of the cross in difficult situations. This material can be used in a variety of contexts including sermons. Part 3 is more practical, providing advice on working with crosses, including making your own, and putting together cross-related worship. It also features the Stations of the Cross with Bible readings and suggestions for making your own Stations. Part 4 deals more particularly with prayer and meditation, and includes information on making the Sign of the Cross, labyrinths, prayer stations and retreats on the streets.

Practical Arrangements

The practical arrangements are dealt with at the beginning of any programme, however long it may last and whatever the purpose. This includes:

- Introduction and clarification of the programme.
- Worship arrangements.
- Available facilities and space, inside and out – for worship, talks, meditation, workshops, meals.
- Timing of breaks for tea or coffee and meals (on retreat some people may prefer to bring refreshments in a flask).
- Toilet facilities.
- Times of silence – whole day or part, and whether this includes meals. Stories from Parts 1 and 2 can be read during a meal if silence is being kept.
- List of times when the facilitator or retreat conductor will be available for private discussion.
- Time to answer any questions, both at the start and at the end.

Resources needed

- Sufficient handouts for programmes, worship, information and material for meditation.
- Crosses and crucifixes to display for talks and use as required.
- Pictures relating to the cross as required (can be in books).
- Bibles, paper and writing material.
- CD-player if music is to be used, with extension lead, and suitable music.
- Equipment to project images on CD-ROM.
- Symbols to be used in worship as indicated – images of Jesus, crosses and crucifixes, candles and matches.
- Workshop material as indicated, and black bags for rubbish.

- Refreshments as required.
- All the necessary utensils and sacramental elements if the Eucharist is to be celebrated, or food for an *agape* meal.

The purchase of this book entitles you to photocopy or print out handouts and worship material, for personal or non-profit use as required for meditation, information, worship and workshops.

Collecting Crosses

There are four options in building up a collection of crosses:

1 Make your own collection over time (many being gifted once your interest is known).
2 Encourage a faith community to make a shared collection.
3 Use personal or borrowed crosses for a one-off occasion.
4 Make crosses from a variety of materials (see Part 3).

The mere fact of asking people to collect crosses stimulates their interest, as they will want to know more about them. In a church you can start by identifying those around you. Some have a special significance, like a processional or altar cross, but others are found on banners, kneelers, statues, woodwork, memorials, clerical vestments, embroidered altar linen and altar frontals; or in pictures, stained-glass windows and wall paintings. While not all can be handled, they help people to understand the place of the cross in faith and worship.

When it comes to collecting crosses, church and cathedral gift shops offer a wide selection in various shapes, sizes and mediums. These include: rosaries; holding, hanging and standing crosses; and bookmarks in paper, tatting, lace, leather, plastic and wood. Crosses are also depicted on mugs, bowls, boxes and ashtrays. All have a story to tell. Places of pilgrimage like Walsingham provide rich pickings to suit every purse. Postcards and pictures are found in art galleries, specialist art shops, museums and religious gift shops, while books can be borrowed from libraries in both the art and religious sections.[1]

3 – St Cuthbert's and Canterbury crosses

The Tau and San Damiano crosses of St Francis are widely available, as are those of St George and St Andrew on badges and flags, and the hand-cast models of historic Irish crosses made in Kinsale, County Cork. Elaborately sculpted Celtic high crosses have survived in many parts of Ireland, Wales, Cornwall and Scotland. Plaster models with explanatory information can be found locally. St Cuthbert's cross graces a range of articles in north-east England, as does the Canterbury cross in the south. The Red Cross, Maltese cross (associated with St John's Ambulance), and Poppy Day cross of Remembrance Sunday are all used in storytelling

Shops and kiosks attached to Roman Catholic and Orthodox churches in Europe and the Middle East provide a more exotic selection, as does the Holy Land. In Latin America, the Philippines, Pacific Islands and Africa, hand-crafted crosses are found in roadside markets and kiosks. These may be made from wire, metal, wood, twigs, bone, animal teeth, porcupine quills, leather, beadwork, glass, pottery, raffia, reeds, ivory, shells, paper and plastic. Some find their way into One World gift shops.

Natural crosses may be found in dead tree-trunks with lateral branches, or on stones lined with mineral deposits. More decorative artistic works made of glass, metal, pottery or perspex add colour and interest; but cross jewellery should have a religious link. The greater the variety, the more one is able to explore the place crosses have in our lives. The simplest can often have the most profound meaning.

Mention must be made of a number of contemporary British artists who have focused on the cross. Craigie Aitchison is renowned for his Calvary paintings, while the Cornish artist Michael Finn has sculpted minimalist crucifixes out of blocks of wood. In contrast, Graham Carey has used hand-forged nails discarded in a Bradford timber yard to depict Christ's Passion. In his ongoing quest to depict icons of the invisible God, Peter Eugene Ball's sculptures of the crucifix and Pietà, made from copper and driftwood from Scottish beaches, grace numerous churches and cathedrals throughout Britain.[2] These, and many others, would provide excellent foci for meditation.[3]

Notes

1 For information on collecting images of Christ, see Janet Hodgson, 2006, *The Faith We See: Working with Images of Christ*, Peterborough: Inspire, Methodist Publishing House, pp. 109–11.

2 Peter Eugene Ball, 1999, *Icons of the Invisible God*, Newark: Chevron Books.

3 For an overview of the cross in modern art in the Western world, see Hans-Ruedi Weber, 1979, *On a Friday Noon*: *Meditations Under the Cross*, London: SPCK, WCC Publications, Wm Eerdmans, pp. 72–7. For the cross in Latin America, pp. 78–9; Asia, pp. 80–2; and Africa, pp. 82–6.

PART 1

CROSSES OVER THE AGES AND AROUND THE WORLD

A display of crosses needs to be set out beforehand, visible to all. Participants can bring their own crosses to add to the display. Examples of the basic forms are needed, with simple illustrations being given in the handout. Reference books with pictures can be used to fill gaps if required, or else images from the CD-ROM are projected onto a wall or screen.

Sample Programme for Input on Crosses and Crucifixes

15 minutes:	Welcome, purpose of our time together, programme outline, practical information, questions.
5 minutes:	Opening worship. A hymn or song can be sung.
5 minutes:	Short talk: 'Early History of Crosses'.
40 minutes:	'Basic Forms of Crosses and the Crucifix' (Handout 1). The facilitator will read through the handout, showing examples of each form of cross where possible.
30 minutes to 1 hour:	Participants are asked to choose a cross from the display and then to meditate on it in a peaceful setting. Questions to consider: Why did I choose this cross? What does it mean to me? Is its origin important?
15 minutes:	Optional sharing in pairs as to the meaning of the selected cross, or else continue in silent meditation.

Extending the Programme

This programme can be extended for a full day by adding further modules as given below. This could be on both 'Images of the False Cross' and/or 'True Images of the Cross'. Handouts can be used as short talks or as material for silent reflection. Images on the CD-ROM can be projected as a complementary way of providing information or as a focus for meditation.

Alternatively, using the pick-and-mix approach, modules can be added from other parts of the book – stories, worship, Bible studies, activities, prayer and meditation. When working with a new theme, time should be allowed for silent reflection. This can be followed by sharing in pairs or in small groups; but some participants may wish to keep silence and this must be respected.

Where appropriate, a display of crosses, or pictures of crosses, relating to a specific theme adds much to the experience, more especially if the crosses can be handled. See Part 3 for appropriate questions. The timing of the programme is flexible, depending on the purpose of the event.

Opening Worship

A large cross or crucifix is placed centrally. Candles can be placed on either side and lit at the start. Soft music can help people to relax.

Christ reconciles us all to God in one body through the cross (Ephesians 2.16).

Leader	We lift high the cross,
All	On which Jesus made himself low.
Leader	We glorify the cross,
All	On which Jesus embraced shame.
Leader	We venerate the cross,
All	On which Jesus hung as a criminal.
Leader	We praise the cross,
All	On which Jesus died for our sins.
Leader	Behold the cross of Jesus,
All	Which reconciles the children of Adam.
Leader	We carry the cross,
All	The source of peace and eternal life. Amen.

Collect for Holy Cross Day (14 September)

Almighty God,
who in the passion of your blessed Son,
made an instrument of shameful death
to be for us the means of life:
grant us so to glory in the cross of Christ
that we may gladly suffer for his sake;
who is alive and reigns with you and the Holy Spirit,
one God, now and for ever. Amen. (England)[1]

Note

1 Collect for Holy Cross Day, *The Alternative Service Book 1980,* pp. 832–3. Copyright © The Central Board of Finance of the Church of England, 1980; The Archbishops' Council, 1999 (by permission).

1

BACKGROUND INFORMATION

Early History of Crosses

Although the cross is the one universally recognized symbol of the Christian faith, the sign dates back to antiquity. The oldest examples are those engraved or painted

on flat pebbles, dating from 10,000 BC, in a cave in the French Pyrenees. These 'ancestor stones' were believed to contain the spirits of the dead. In Africa and Scandinavia crosses are found on Bronze Age rock engravings, while pre-Christian crosses and even crucifixions were widely depicted in both Eastern and Western cultures right across the world.

Exactly when the cross became a symbol of Christ's sacrifice is uncertain. Nor was it always a symbol of the Christian faith. In one of the catacombs, the figure on the cross has the head of a jackass, graffiti by a sceptical Roman soldier. Over the ages the cross has served as a protective talisman, an object of veneration, a sign of military might, a tool in rites of exorcism, and as a piece of jewellery. We need to be

4 – Traditional cross shapes

judicious in its use because, as the ultimate sign of the redemptive suffering of God, it should represent simplicity and holy poverty.

The New Testament uses two different words to denote the cross as an instrument of torture on which Jesus died. More common is the word *stauros* meaning an upright pale or stick. The other word is *xulon*, referred to in Acts 5.30, 10.39, 13.29, Galatians 3.13, and 1 Peter 2.24. It simply means anything made of wood, a timber beam or staff, or, indirectly, a tree. It was probably an optional word for the tree of death (the cross) in contrast to the tree of life, as used in Revelation 2.7: 'To everyone who conquers, I will give permission to eat from the tree of life that is in the paradise of God.' Other references include Revelation 22.2, 14, 19.

One can assume that Jesus carried the crossbeam and not the entire cross. During Roman times vertical stakes were set permanently in the ground at Calvary to which crosspieces were affixed horizontally with ropes or nails at the time of crucifixion. Identifying the instrument of Jesus' death with a two-beamed cross was sealed permanently with the Vulgate's Latin rendering of both *stauros* and *xulon* with the word *crux*, from which is derived 'cross' in English and the German *Kreuz*. Up until the tenth century, the English referred to the cross as the 'rood'.

Inculturation of the Cross

Inculturation is the term commonly used to describe the ongoing dialogue between the form in which the gospel is presented and the symbols of the receiving culture. This process has been taking place ever since Christianity first took root in Europe. Over the centuries, the people themselves, not the institutional Church, have taken the initiative in drawing on indigenous thought patterns, imagery, myth, symbolism, customs and traditions to establish their own expressions of their new-found faith and to relate it to their everyday experiences. Celtic Christianity is one example, folk religion another.

Just as the four Gospels show how the word of God was presented so as to resonate with people living in quite different contexts, so, too, will contemporary expressions of the faith take on new forms. The receiving cultures could be far distant countries. Or, as in Britain, the pioneering movement known as 'fresh expressions of church' has sought to reach out to the neglected margins of society. Here, networks based on relationships rather than a gathered congregation could be made among the youth or the elderly, in pubs, cafés, offices, factories, schools, sports arenas, shopping centres or housing estates. But in every instance, it is they who will determine what will be retained symbolically of their old way of life and what will be transformed by the gospel to meet new needs.[1]

The many faces of the Hebrew Jesus found in the wide variety of cultures around the world are a classic example of this process. So, too, are the innumerable variations in the design and shape of crosses, which have developed over time according to different cultural influences and life-changing historic events, both national and personal. Thus, while the one and only cross of Christ symbolizes a spiritual dimension common to the faith of all Christians, the many stylistic variations exemplify the ongoing process of inculturation over the ages unique to every culture and tradition.

Handout 1
Basic Forms of Crosses and the Crucifix

Over time, crosses have taken on an enormous variety of shapes and styles, but there are four basic forms.[2]

1. Most common in the West is the **Latin cross** (*crux immisa*) with its vertical bar crossed two-thirds of the way up by a single horizontal beam. The geometric design of the Latin cross is much like its Islamic counterpart, but whereas the latter testifies to the totally transcendent character of Allah, the former proclaims the incarnational God of the Gospels. Thanks to its economy of lines, the Latin cross symbolizes both the Incarnation and the *kenosis*, or self-emptying, of Jesus.

5 – Latin cross

2. The **Greek cross** (*crux quadrata)* has equilateral arms intersecting in the middle, early examples being found on gravestones in the catacombs of Rome, Malta and Jerusalem. Eastern Orthodox Christians were particularly attracted to its symmetrical shape. Since the fourth century, both Latin and Greek crosses have greatly influenced the architectural and decorative styles of church buildings and ecclesiastical heraldry.

6 – Greek cross

7– Ethiopian crosses

The intricately designed **Ethiopian cross** is an early derivation of the Greek cross, being carried on a long processional staff and used by priests to bless the faithful. Scarves are attached to the crosses, showing regional differences. Ethiopian women not only wear the cross but have them on their faces too. They are a symbol of both Christ's death and the wellspring of life.

With origins going back to the Neolithic period in Eurasia, the **swastika** is a Greek-style equilateral cross with its arms bent at right angles either to the right or to the left. The swastika has long been a sacred symbol in Dharmic religions in the East, in Hinduism, Buddhism and Jainism, its widespread use on ancient monuments testifying to its antiquity. It also appeared on artefacts in pre-Christian cultures in Europe and the Americas. In Christian usage, the swastika is found in catacombs and mosaics in early churches and is sometimes hooked. Only after its appropriation by the Nazi Party in Germany did it come into disrepute.

8 – Traditional swastika cross and right-facing decorative Hindu form

3. The **Tau cross** (*crux commissa*) takes its name from the last letter of the Hebrew alphabet, which was transcribed as the letter T in the Greek alphabet, and was the emblem of St Anthony of Egypt. It was the sign made by the Israelites on their doorposts at the Exodus to symbolize being under God's protection, and was also used by Moses in raising the Brazen Serpent. *Commissa* means joined or attached.

9 – Tau cross

The **Ankh**, consisting of an oval loop on top of a letter T (the Tau), was the Egyptian hieroglyphic character that symbolized both the preserving of life and eternal life, and is associated with deities. It was revered by Coptic Christians as an icon possessing mystical power, symbolizing life after death. It may have influenced the Celtic cross too as Celtic traditions blended with ancient symbols from the East independent of Rome.

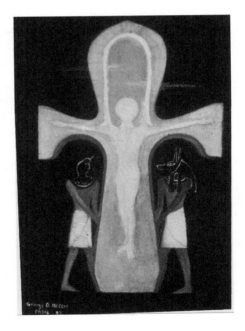

10 – Jesus inside an Ankh

4. The fourth basic form, **St Andrew's cross** (*crux decussata*), is derived from the Latin numeral for 10, X (*decem*). St Andrew is the patron saint of Scotland, Greece and Russia. In the shape of the Greek letter *chi*, the first letter for Christ, it was another disguised form of the cross used by early Christians. Known as the Saltire cross in heraldic design, it appears on many national flags in different forms and colours, often representing the Christian faith of bygone kings. The format of the Scottish flag dates from the ninth century when a cross made by white clouds in a blue sky was regarded by King Angus as a good omen prior to winning a decisive battle.

11 – St Andrew's cross

The earliest example of a **crucifix**, with the figure or corpus of Christ nailed to a cross, dates from the late sixth century. Crucifixes emphasize the sacrifice of Jesus and are commonly used as an object of veneration. Whereas the corpora of Eastern Orthodox Churches tend to show Jesus already dead, Roman Catholics have focused on the suffering Christ, the exact imagery changing over time. In the Romanesque period, it is about the peace and salvation wrought by Christ's sacrifice, rather than his agony. With the medieval realism of the thirteenth century, the emphasis moved to the humanity of Jesus and his redeeming sacrifice with the crucifix showing his bleeding, tortured body crowned with thorns. Two centuries later, the more optimistic Renaissance artists portrayed Christ as a serene figure with head bowed and eyes closed. Protestant churches concentrate on the empty cross, denoting the resurrected Christ. Their crucifixes depict a robed and triumphant risen Christ with arms raised, often surrounded by rays of light.

12 – Traditional crucifix

Handout 2
Orthodox Examples

The many variations in shape and design provide intriguing insights into church history and folk religion as, for example, the three-barred **Russian crucifix**. It has an upper horizontal bar representing the plaque with Pontius Pilate's Latin inscription, INRI, *Iesus Nazarenus Rex Iudaeorum*, 'Jesus the Nazarean, King of the Jews'. The second bar represents Jesus' outstretched arms, with the lowest one, his footrest, always diagonally slanted. An eleventh-century tradition regards the latter as a judgement scale, with the penitent thief, St Dismas, finding salvation and being angled upward towards heaven, while the impenitent thief, Gestas, is being sent downward to hell. In Russian literature, Christ is said to lift his right foot to lighten the sins of believers while casting disbelievers into hell with the left. Yet another tradition links the diagonal slant with the X-shaped cross of St Andrew.

13 – The Eastern cross

When a monk or nun is professed in the Orthodox Church, he or she is given a knotted cord finished with a cross and tassel. The Greeks call this a *komwschoinion* (knotted cord), and the Russians, a *tchotki* (from the verb 'to count'). The cord is associated with the recitation of the Jesus Prayer – 'Lord Jesus Christ, Son of God, have mercy upon me, a sinner' – and is used to aid concentration. It is made of two strands of black wool woven together to make either 50 or 100 knots. The strands represent the unity and duality inherent in all creation – light and dark, good and evil, male and female, soul and body – culminating in the cross. As with the painting of an icon, the weaving of a prayer rope is in itself a prayer.

Bible Study or Reflection

'But we proclaim Christ crucified, a stumbling block to Jews and foolishness to Gentiles' (1 Corinthians 1.23). Yet to believers the cross is a sign of God's mysterious power made perfect in weakness and his wisdom made manifest through folly.

- How would you explain the meaning of the cross to a non-Christian in non-churchy language?
- Reflect on the difference between a cross and a crucifix. How has this influenced your spirituality?
- What do you feel about non-Christians wearing crosses as jewellery, or about a Christian being punished for wearing a cross to work?
- Think about a cross you have seen somewhere and how it affected you – in a church, cathedral or cemetery; picture, sculpture or film; in someone's home, on the internet, as a roadside memorial, or at a historic site.

Notes

1 For information on the many faces of Christ and inculturation, see Hodgson, *The Faith We See*.

2 For further information, see Heather Child and Dorothy Colles, 1971, *Christian Symbols Ancient and Modern: A Handbook for Students*, London: G. Bell & Sons. See also internet sources.

2

IMAGES OF THE FALSE CROSS

The Crusading and the Crucified Church – Introduction

As we look back on the history of the Church we are mortified by how our missionary forebears allowed the humble cross of Jesus to become the handmaid of the Crown: how the Church became complicit in the Western European enterprise of slavery, colonialism and neo-colonialism. This is what we call the Crusading Church.

Just as we Christians distinguish between true and false religions, and true and false prophets, so we need to differentiate between true and false crosses. The cross points to persecution, but of itself this does not make for Christian martyrdom. As St Augustine said, 'What makes a martyr is not suffering but the cause.' Jesus himself warns that 'the hour will come in which the one who kills you will think he is doing something pleasing to God' (John 16.2). Indeed, those who kill prophets and defenders of justice venerate the false cross, leading to oppression and suffering. In contrast, the true cross of Christian martyrs is about redemption and healing, and creates a crucified Church.

Handout 3
The Emperor Constantine

Our story begins in the fourth century with the Emperor Constantine, who, before a battle against Germanic tribes, had a vision of a luminous cross coupled with the words '*In hoc signe vinces*' ('In this sign conquer'). The Emperor regarded this vision as a blessing, vindicating conquest and killing; and victory turned him into a believer. Under his patronage, Christianity, the once radical creed of revolutionaries, became the religion of the state, with the cross featuring on the Imperial standard. The establishment of Constantinople as the Emperor's capital in Byzantium gave the highly stylized figures of the Byzantine cross its name. As the evangelization of Europe was driven by military might rather than spiritual persuasion, the cross became a symbol of triumphalism representing the power of the Roman Empire.

An old tradition relates that St Helena, Constantine's mother, journeyed to the Holy Land and discovered the original cross on which Jesus supposedly had died. Her cross is said to have been encrusted with precious stones, not only enhancing the devotion of the faithful but stimulating the symbolic use of the cross in art and sumptuous ornamentation as in baroque churches. Known as the *crux gemmata*, these gemmed crosses, inlaid with gold, are favoured by the likes of footballers, entertainers and celebrities, making a mockery of the Christian faith.

Handout 4
Crosses of the Crusaders

Between the eleventh and thirteenth centuries, the cross of the Crusaders represents another false cross. Coming mostly from Western Europe, the Crusaders marched under the Christian banner, taking their name from the cross which they bore on their clothing and heraldry. The first crosses were blood-red on white, but over time different armies adopted distinguishing variations of shape and colour. The **Jerusalem cross**, also known as the Crusaders' cross, consists of one large cross with four smaller ones in the four quadrants. This is variously interpreted as Christ with the four evangelists, the five wounds of Jesus on the cross (four for the hands and feet and one for the spear wound in his side), and the gospel being taken by missionaries to the four corners of the world.

14 – The Crusaders' or Jerusalem cross

When the Crusaders invaded Palestine, they targeted not only Muslims but also Jews and Orthodox Christians, who, ironically, had enjoyed civil peace under Muslim rule. To this day the anti-Islamic image of the Crusaders' cross still haunts Christianity in the Middle East. Others see it as an emblem of anti-Semitism, or of the Great Schism within the Church between the West and Orthodox East.

Palestine is also associated with the veneration of St George, the legendary warrior saint supposedly martyred at the end of the third century. The Crusaders brought his red cross on a white ground back to England to become the country's national flag, while he became its patron saint. The contemporary popularity of the flag has been generated by nationalistic fervour in football, with the British Nationalist Party co-opting the power of this imagery as a fascist symbol of white Britishness. It must be distinguished from the emblem of the International Red Cross, founded to aid the wounded in battle, whose red arms do not reach the edges.

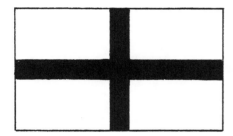 

15 – St George's cross and Red Cross

Handout 5
Columbus and the Conquistadores

A few centuries later we have the cross of explorers, such as Christopher 'the Christbearer' Columbus, celebrated for their heroic deeds in 'discovering' distant lands. In search of treasure, they pursued the myth of bringing the light of Christ to 'benighted savages'. The invaders not only destroyed ancient civilizations, but their legacy of disease, slavery, and exploitation resulted in genocide on a horrendous scale.

After his entry into the Bay of Hispaniola, Columbus told his patron, the King of Spain, '[I] placed a very tall cross at the harbour's entrance, a very visible mount, as a sign that the land belongs to your Highness and especially as a sign of Jesus

Christ and the honour of Christianity.'[1] Columbus claimed protection from the Holy Trinity from whom he hoped for victory. Neither he, the king nor the Church saw any contradiction in the cross of Christ being used to sanction the conquest of 'sinful unbelievers', much to the detriment of Christian mission.

Posing as ambassadors of Christ, wave after wave of Conquistadores plundered the New World to acquire enormous wealth. For the indigenous people, the missionary activity of the foreigners was marked by military persecution, pillage and rape, with whole tribes being totally decimated. The Dominican monk Bartolomé de las Casas was a lone voice in denouncing the atrocities. Protesting to the Spanish king that Jesus Christ was crucified hourly in the crucified local people, and that the behaviour of the Spaniards 'would become the Crescent far better than the spotless Cross', he was promptly recalled home.[2]

16 – Arriving missionaries

Whereas the Conquistadores conquered the lands and bodies of their victims, the majority of missionaries in the eighteenth and nineteenth centuries attempted to subjugate the minds of indigenous peoples across the world by denouncing their traditional cultures and spiritual practices as heathen and satanic. With the cross of Christ now inextricably linked with Western civilization, Jesus was presented as a white Saviour together with a Eurocentric gospel. Indigenous expressions of Christianity were rejected as syncretistic heresies. No wonder that the term 'missionary' has received such a bad press in recent years despite their sacrificial ministries.

Modern Examples of the False Cross

The Nazis under Adolf Hitler usurped the ancient, sacred Hindu symbol of the swastika (meaning 'spiritual wellbeing' in Sanskrit) and distorted the traditional form of its right-angled arms to bend anti-clockwise instead of clockwise. Whereas the Old Testament saw the Hebrews as the chosen people of God, and the cross of Jesus affirmed his followers as the new chosen people, the Nazi hooked cross (*Hakenkreuz*) represented the Germanic people as the chosen master race and the Hebrews as the unredeemed. Their cross stood for an Aryan Jesus exulting in unbridled power, with the Lutheran Church being co-opted as an instrument of their nationalistic creed.

The burning cross of the Ku Klux Klan is an extension of the Nazi swastika and an emblem of the superiority of the so-called 'white Christian civilization' over Catholics, blacks, Jews, etc. In a less strident tone, the Dutch Reformed Church of the apartheid government in South Africa preached the hegemony of whites over blacks under such a cross.

Jürgen Moltmann sums up the transgressions of those in power over the ages: 'The Church has much abused the theology of the cross and the mysticism of the passion in the interest of those who cause suffering.'[3] Too often, indigenous people, slaves and peasants had been called upon by the Church to accept suffering as 'their cross' without rebelling. What the overlords needed was an understanding of the true meaning of the cross to free them from their pride and liberate their victims.

In working with crosses, we need to remember the way in which false images of the cross have distorted the gospel down the centuries. These ghosts of the past must be exorcized by presenting true images of the cross.

Images of the False Cross in Film – Discussion

The film *The Mission* (Roland Joffe, 1986) recalls the Church's past in Latin America. After watching it, contrast the role of the non-violent priest with that of the Cardinal in deciding the fate of the Indian mission under the colonial onslaught. How does this illustrate the difference between true and false images of the cross?

Notes

1 Cited by Luis N. Riviera, 1991, in *A Violent Evangelism: The Political and Religious Conquest of the Americas*, Louisville: John Knox Press, p. 8.

2 Cited from a missive to Carlos/Charles I in 1542.

3 Jürgen Moltmann, translated by John Bowden and R. A. Wilson, 1974, *The Crucified God*, New York: Harper and Row, p. 43.

3

TRUE IMAGES OF THE CROSS

Saints and Their Crosses

Display as many of the crosses of saints as possible where visible to all, or else focus just on those you will be discussing.

Worship to Honour the Saints of God

'Because he [Christ] himself was tested by what he suffered, he is able to help those who are being tested' (Hebrews 2.18).

Leader	Let us bless the Lord God,
All	and also his saints.
Leader	We give thanks for their life and work,
All	and ask God for courage to follow in their footsteps.
Leader	Praise God, for he is good and just.
All	He is just because we are all his saints. Amen

Inscription on Bede's tomb, Galilee chapel, Durham Cathedral

Christ is the morning star
Who when the night of this world is past
Brings to his Saints
The promise of the light of life
And opens everlasting day.

The saints are associated with some of the most popular images of the true cross; and their stories continue to inspire their many followers around the world to take up the cross and live holy and simple lives. A few examples suffice, some better known than others.

Handout 6
St Francis

Probably the most well known of the saints' crosses are the **Tau** and the **San Damiano Crucifix** of St Francis of Assisi. The Tau, known too as the **Cross of St Anthony the Hermit, of Egypt,** was chosen by St Francis after working with the followers of St Anthony in caring for lepers. They used this ancient symbol as a talisman against skin diseases and the plague. For St Francis it represented life-long fidelity to the Passion of Christ, and affirmed his pledge to serve the least, the leper and outcast of his day. He signed his letters with the Tau, wrote it on the walls of his cell, and told his friars that, with their arms outstretched, the shape of their religious habit conformed to the Tau. This was to be a constant reminder of their lifelong commitment to incarnate the compassion of God. Today, this cross is commonly worn by Franciscans, both religious and Third Order laity.

The St Damiano Crucifix is the one St Francis was praying before in 1205 when he received God's commission to 'Go and repair my house'. Painted during the twelfth century in Umbria, the artist is unknown but was possibly a Syrian monk as reflected in the Byzantine iconography. The original cross was about six feet high and four feet wide, and painted on walnut wood to which cloth had been glued. As an icon of the transfigured Christ, its aim was to impart the meaning of Christ's Passion, death, resurrection and ascension into glory, so strengthening the faith of believers.[1]

Initially, St Francis thought that he had been called to rebuild the ruined and

17 – San Damiano cross

abandoned San Damiano chapel only, but later realized that his vocation was to transform the Catholic Church itself. During his lifetime, St Clare and her community of Poor Clare Sisters, a contemplative order in the Franciscan tradition, lived in the chapel. The original crucifix now hangs in their convent, the Basilica of St Clare (the thirteenth-century Santa Chiara church) in nearby Assisi.

Prayer of St Francis of Assisi

We adore you, O Christ, and we praise you, because by your holy cross, you have redeemed the world.
All-highest, glorious God, cast your light into the darkness of my heart.
Give me right faith, firm hope, perfect charity and profound humility, with wisdom and perception, O Lord, so that I may do what is truly your holy will. Amen.

Handout 7
St Dominic

St Dominic (1170–1221) was a Spanish contemporary and friend of St Francis, and founder of the Friars Preachers or Dominican Order of Preachers (OP). He established his scholastic Order in southern France to preach the gospel and combat heresy among the Cathars, from where it expanded to Spain and beyond. The Order was marked by poverty, charity and intellectual rigour, its motto being 'to praise, to bless, to preach'. Renowned for its academic tradition, it produced a succession of leading theologians and philosophers, with a less glorious role in the Inquisition.

Prayer and contemplation are integral to the mystical spirituality of the Order, and St Dominic's devotion to the Virgin Mary encouraged the widespread use of the Rosary. In 1221, a Dominican community was founded in Oxford. Known as Blackfriars (as in Blackfriars Bridge, London), they wore a black cloak or mantle over a white habit, representing truth over heresy. The Dominican cross is a black and white striped Latin cross with a *fleur de lis* on the end of each arm, recalling their French beginnings. Their Greek-shaped Gyronny cross is also black and white, the white reflecting 'the joy and purity of Christ', while the black is a reminder 'of their humility and obligation for penance'.[2]

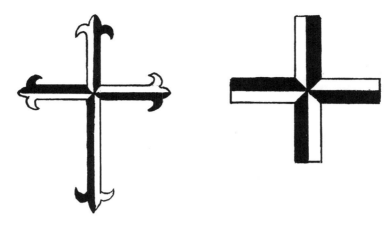

18 – Two Dominican crosses

Prayer of St Dominic

May God the Father who made us bless us.
May God the Son send his healing among us.
May God the Holy Spirit move within us and
give us eyes to see with, ears to hear with,
and hands that your work might be done.
May we walk and preach the word of God to all.
May the angel of peace watch over us and
lead us at last by God's grace to the Kingdom. Amen.

Handout 8
St Andrew and St Peter

The X-shaped cross of St Andrew recalls his martyrdom in Greece during the reign of Emperor Nero, the first-century Apostle believing himself unworthy to be crucified like Christ. For the same reason, St Peter chose to be crucified on an upside-down Latin cross. However, the Vatican uses two crossed keys as its official insignia in remembrance of those given to Peter by Christ to open the doors of paradise. Any crosses which are associated with the martyrdom of saints are effective in inspiring service, humility, sacrifice and justice.

St Thomas or Syrian Cross

The St Thomas or Syrian cross dates back to the seventh or eighth century and is associated with the St Thomas Christians of Kerala, South India, who are closely linked with the Syrian Orthodox Church. Because the stone cross never carries the effigy of Christ, it symbolizes life and resurrection rather than the suffering and death of Jesus. Rich in Indian symbols relating to the Apostle's ministry, it is topped by the image of a dove representing the Holy Spirit, while the four points end in buds, rather than trefoils or florets, indicating the believer's faith in the flowering of new life. This sermon in stone speaks of the virtues of patience in the face of adversity, and of God's never-failing providence, two qualities which doubting Thomas lacked.

St Thomas' cross is mounted on a full-blown lotus flower symbolic of Hindu–Buddhist spirituality. In Hindu iconography, the lotus represents enlightenment, detachment and purity in the midst of the hurly-burly of life and is regarded as a holy offering to God. Below the lotus is a three-stepped pyramid symbolizing the mount of Calvary. It may also represent the holy pit where sacrificial fires burn and where ritual offerings are made according to Hindu iconography. An obvious example of inculturation, this Christian cross is matched with the comparable Hindu theme of *yajna*, the holy sacrifice.

Celtic Crosses

Handout 9
Irish Solar and Standing Crosses

Celtic culture was highly receptive to Christianity and its emblems were readily incorporated with new adaptations in an even older process of inculturation. The traditional Celtic cross is a Latin cross with a circle or ring in the centre. Among the more likely interpretations of the ring are the symbolism of the sun god, a Tau cross with a looped top (like the Egyptian Ankh), or a cosmic wheel. The sun was worshipped as a deity by the early Celts and its symbol together with crosses are engraved on pagan pillar-stones and Bronze Age burial urns. Incarnated as an indigenous expression of Christianity, the Celtic cross incorporates 'the symbolism of the circle of creation held in tension with the cross of redemption'.[3] However, the Irish Solar cross is nearly always the Easter cross, representing the victorious risen Christ 'who rules over the earth and humankind as radiantly as the sun'.[4]

19 – Sun cross

A popular myth has St Patrick introducing the Celtic cross into Ireland by combining the Christian cross with the lifegiving symbol of the sun to facilitate the conversion of his pagan followers. But the design of the Solar cross is much older than that, similar 'sun crosses' dating back to Bronze Age Europe. The circle has many Christian interpretations including a halo, crown of thorns, the world for which Christ died, his resurrection, and a symbol of eternity.

In early Christian Ireland a wooden or stone cross would generally be found outside a church, and some liturgical rites would be carried out there by both the monks and the local community.[5] The Celtic standing-stone crosses, dating from the seventh or eighth century on, were yet another medium for translating the gospel into contemporary cultural forms, with significant elements of the pre-Christian standing stones and giant prehistoric megaliths being transformed by the incoming culture of the Church to express the Celts' new-found faith. The stone crosses, mounted on a pyramid base and up to 15 feet in height, were erected by missionaries to mark preaching stations and monasteries. Their usage spread from Ireland to Wales, Cornwall, Northumbria, Scotland and the Scottish Isles, and they were numbered in their hundreds. Many

20 – Early Celtic cross

have survived, some preserved in heritage centres like Clonmacnoise on the River Shannon in Ireland, or in museums.

The elaborate carvings which covered the rectangular shaft as well as the arms of the standing cross could include inscriptions in Scandinavian runes, Saxon uncials and complex Celtic designs, together with Christian imagery. These decorations reflected the deep mysticism of the Celtic monks and their belief in the presence of God in all creation. Similarly, intricate depictions of the cross are found in illuminated manuscripts such as the Lindisfarne Gospels, the purpose of this iconography being to teach. The carvings could include familiar stories from the Old and New Testaments as well as the lives of saints. The fall and redemption are recurring themes, as is the idea of sacrifice, while the crucifixion or Christ the reigning king invariably takes centre place of each immense, circled cross. As De Waal explains, 'these great high crosses stand as a public proclamation of the faith, crying aloud their message: God helps the faithful, God rescues his people from death and oppression'.[6]

The Celtic cross stood for three different kinds of martyrdom: red, white and green. Red martyrdom, signifying blood and death, represented the physical, social and political oppression suffered by people in the form of slavery, slaughter, rape and pillage. White martyrdom was the bloodless alternative open to hermits who took refuge in remote hideaways such as islands, hilltops and forests. Devoting themselves to a life of penance and prayer, their aim was to emulate Christ in his vulnerability on the cross, and share in his dependence on divine guidance and succour. Green martyrdom was played out in the interior life by a letting go of the ego in the manner of a spiritual warrior. The symbolism of the Celtic Solar cross is missed when we follow New Age sensibilities in stressing the circle and not the cross.

21 – Celtic cross

Handout 10
St Brigid's Cross

St Brigid's cross (St Bridget, St Briget, Cros Bhrighite) is a memorial to the only indigenous patron saint of Ireland. Her feast day falls on 1 February, commemorating her death around AD 525. Traditionally, schoolchildren make her cross on that day to celebrate the start of spring. Revered as 'Mary of the Gaels', and patron saint of crafts, poets and healers, Brigid founded the first convent, in Kildare, around AD 470. Over time, folklore added to her fame with stories of her generosity and miraculous feats, such as being able to provide a constant flow of milk and ale to her visitors.

Legend has it that St Brigid's father was either a pagan chieftain, or, at least, of the tax-paying class. As he lay dying, she sat beside him in prayer while weaving a cross from the rushes on the floor, strewn there for warmth and cleanliness. Her father asked about the meaning of the cross and was so overwhelmed by the story of Christ's Passion that he was baptized before his death.

In Ireland, St Brigid's cross is made of rushes, pulled rather than cut, in the shape of a swastika, suggesting pre-Christian influence. Drawing on ancient beliefs, it is believed to protect people and animals from sickness, fire, evil and want, and is hung in rafters or above the entrances to dwellings – cottages, pubs and stables.

Prayer of St Brigid of Gael

I arise today
through a mighty strength;
God's power to guide me,
God's might to uphold me,
God's eyes to watch over me;
God's ear to hear me,
God's word to give me speech,
God's hand to guard me,
God's way to lie before me,
God's shield to shelter me,
God's host to secure me.

22 – St Brigid's cross

Making a St Brigid's Cross

Although the cross is traditionally made from rushes, straw does just as well, as do reeds, pipe-cleaners, raffia, or plastic drinking straws. The number of straws required varies from nine to sixteen. Rubber-bands, twine or ribbon are used to tie up the four ends, which are then trimmed evenly. Customarily, all materials are blessed before construction. Step-by-step instructions with illustrations are found on the internet (see illustration above and picture on CD-ROM):

- http://iol.ie/-scphadr/makecross.html
- http://www.ehow.com/how_5157619_make-saint-brigids-cross.html
- http://www.ipcc.ie/bicartpr3.html
- http://www.fisheaters.com/stbrigidscross.html
- http://www.geocities.com/rainforest/vines/5863/cmethod1.html (three traditional methods offered).

Handout 11
St Cuthbert

St Cuthbert was a Celtic Christian with Scottish roots, being born around AD 634 near the Tweed in the Northumbrian kingdom. As a shepherd boy, he had a mystical vision of the soul of St Aidan, Bishop of Lindisfarne, being carried up to heaven by angels. Interpreting this as a call to be a missionary, he entered the monastery of Old Melrose to be trained in the Irish tradition with much prayer, fasting and studying. He went on to become guest master at Ripon, and then Prior of Lindisfarne, where, after the Synod of Whitby in 664, he had some difficulty in reconciling his community to accept the Roman rites.

Renowned as a man of prayer, Cuthbert was reputed to have the gift of healing, drawing a large following. In 676 his desire for the solitary life led him to become a hermit on Inner Farne island. But in 685, he was reluctantly persuaded to leave his austere retreat and become Bishop of Lindisfarne, his missionary journeys now taking him all

23 – St Cuthbert's cross

over Northumbria. Two years later he returned to Inner Farne to die.[7] He was buried at Lindisfarne, but following the Danish invasion, his monks criss-crossed the north-east, carrying his wooden coffin until they finally settled on the eventual site of Durham Cathedral. Legend relates that when his burial casket was opened later, his body was found perfectly preserved, this apparent miracle fostering his cult status as a saint. In 1104 his tomb was reopened and his relics removed to a shrine behind the high altar of the newly completed cathedral. Legendary happenings led to his being regarded as protector of his northern 'people of the saint'.

When St Cuthbert's coffin was opened once again in 1827, his pectoral cross was found deeply buried in his robes on his breast. Made of gold and embellished with garnets, the Saxon cross follows the Greek style with four equal arms. Early Celtic influence has also given it the name of Thor's cross because each arm is splayed with a Thor-like hammer head. The cross later became a heraldic emblem in the arms of Durham and Newcastle universities, and is revered by his many followers.

Irish Penal Cross

The Irish penal cross, resembling a short-armed crucifix, exemplifies a Crucified Church. This folk art harks back to the penal days in Ireland when Catholic religion was suppressed by its Protestant rulers. Its streamlined shape allowed the cross to be hidden up a sleeve. Embellished with symbols of the Passion, such as a cock and a pot representing the resurrection, they were used as pilgrimage crosses in connection with Lough Derg during the seventeenth and eighteenth centuries.

24 – Irish penal cross

Compostela, Maltese and Coventry Crosses

Handout 12
The Way of St James the Great to Santiago de Compostela

The Way of St James the Great, also known as St James the Apostle, to Santiago de Compostela in north-western Spain, is also embedded in pagan origins. This includes a Celtic death journey towards the setting sun beyond Cape Finisterre. As

25 – St James the Great's cross

an important pilgrimage route in medieval times, the Way competed with the arduous journey to Jerusalem or Rome in earning a plenary indulgence. The scallop shell, washed up in abundance on the Galician shores, provided proof of completion of the journey. Apart from its practical usage for drinking and eating, the grooved shell symbolized God's guiding hand, like the waves of the sea, leading pilgrims to the tomb of the Apostle at Compostela.

Thousands of pilgrims still follow the Way from different starting points in France and Spain, culminating in a Mass in the cathedral at journey's end. As the patron saint of Spain, St James' cross is also called the Spanish cross or the cross of the Knights of Santiago, the knights being a military order to protect pilgrims to the shrine. The cross may bear a heart-like ornament on top, but is shaped according to a flory or fitched cross, the lower part being pointed like a sword blade or spear. As the cross of a warrior, it symbolized taking up the sword in the name of Christ and was popularized by the Crusaders. The cross was stuck upright in the ground so that pilgrims could kneel before it during their daily devotions.

26 – Cross of the Order of Santiago

The Maltese Cross

The Maltese cross is yet another cross with Crusader links, originating with the Knights of St John, a military and religious order in Jerusalem. They had an eight-pointed, flayed-edge white cross on a black background. The eight points represent the eight beatitudes in Jesus' Sermon on the Mount (Matthew 5.3–10). They also represent the eight leagues of the Order, while the four main sections of the cross symbolize the four cardinal virtues: fortitude, justice, temperance and perseverance. The white denotes purity, the knights being sworn to chastity, poverty and obedience. It became known as the Maltese cross when the Order moved to Malta in 1530 to concentrate on hospital care. The cross is known in Britain as the emblem of the St John's Ambulance Brigade.

27 – Maltese cross

Coventry Cathedral Cross of Nails

The cross of nails from Coventry Cathedral is a good example of the contemporary Church's ministry in working towards reconciliation worldwide. After being bombed on 14 November 1940 during the Second World War, the new cathedral was built alongside the ruins of the old one as both a celebration of twentieth-century art and architecture, and as witness to the Christian belief that sacrifice is followed by resurrection. The high altar cross was inspired by the charred cross in the cathedral ruins, while two charred beams which had fallen in the shape of a cross were placed on the old altar. Another cross was made by binding three medieval nails from the burnt roof trusses to become a symbol of peace and reconciliation. After the war, such crosses were donated to German cities flattened by Allied bombing, leading to lasting partnerships with Berlin, Kiel and Dresden. There are now 160 Cross of Nails Centres around the world, encouraging people to work towards peace and reconciliation within their own communities. A service using a Litany of Reconciliation is held in the ruins of the old cathedral every Friday at noon.

28 – Coventry Cathedral cross

Closing Prayers

The Cross from a Tenth-Century African Hymn

The cross is the way of the lost.
The cross is the staff of the lame.
The cross is the guide of the blind.
The cross is the strength of the weak.
The cross is the hope of the hopeless.
The cross is the freedom of the slaves.
The cross is the water of the seeds.
The cross is the consolation of the bonded labourers.
The cross is the source of those who seek water.
The cross is the cloth of the naked.

Prayer of St Teresa of Avila (1515–82)

Christ has no body now on earth but yours,
No hands but yours,
No feet but yours.
Yours are the only eyes
through which his compassion can shine forth upon a troubled world,
yours are the only feet
with which he can go about the world,
and yours are the hands
with which he is to bless us now. Amen

Notes

1 The rich symbolism in the San Damiano Crucifix is analysed at the website http://www.franciscanfriarstor.com/stfrancis/stf_san_damiano_cross.htm.

2 Paul Harding, 2009, 'Dominican Cross', www.seiyaku.com.

3 Based on information provided by Esther De Waal, 1991, *Every Earthly Blessing: Celebrating a Spirituality of Creation*, Ann Arbor, Michigan: Servant Publications, p. 118.

4 Anton Wessels, 1994, *Europe: Was It Ever Really Christian? The Interaction Between Gospel and Culture*, London: SCM Press (translated from Dutch), p. 76. For information on Celtic crosses, see the internet.

5 Based on De Waal, p. 117.

6 De Waal, p. 121. For further information on high crosses, see pp. 118–22.

7 *Bede: The Ecclesiastical History of the English People*, edited by Judith McClure and Roger Collins, 1994, New York: Oxford University Press, pp. 223–33, 236–7, 361.

PART 2

LIVING THE CROSS

4

BIG CROSS, LITTLE CROSSES

<table>
<tr><td colspan="2">Programme for a Half-Day or Evening Session (flexible timing)</td></tr>
<tr><td>15 minutes:</td><td>Gather for refreshments and a chat.</td></tr>
<tr><td>10 minutes:</td><td>Welcome and introduction to the programme.</td></tr>
<tr><td>5 minutes:</td><td>Opening worship.</td></tr>
<tr><td>15 minutes:</td><td>Introductory talk on 'Big Cross, Little Crosses'.</td></tr>
<tr><td>15 minutes:</td><td>Reflection on Handout 13.</td></tr>
<tr><td>15 minutes:</td><td>Tea break.</td></tr>
<tr><td>45 minutes:</td><td>Bible study No. 1.</td></tr>
<tr><td>30 minutes:</td><td>Share in pairs if desired, or continue with silent meditation.</td></tr>
</table>

Closure.

Or if part of a full-day programme, then time will be taken for a midday act of worship followed by a lunch.

Break and rest period. Bible study, sharing and reflection can all be extended.

Opening Worship

Place a large cross in the centre, with a few standing little crosses on either side. You can have lit candles alongside too.

'Grace to you and peace from God our Father and the Lord Jesus Christ, who gave himself for our sins to set us free from the present evil age, according to the will of our God and Father, to whom be the glory for ever and ever. Amen (Galatians 1.3–5).

Leader	Rejoice in the cross on which Christ died,
All	So that we may inherit eternal life.
Leader	Glory to the cross of Jesus which won us forgiveness,
All	So that we may forgive one another.
Leader	Hail the cross of Jesus which brought us love,
All	So that we may love one another.
Leader	Amen to the cross of Jesus which gave us peace,
All	So that we may love one another.
Leader	Uphold the cross of Jesus where we found justice,
All	So that we may spread justice around the world.
Leader	Let us embrace the cross on which Jesus suffered,
All	So that we may suffer for his Kingdom. Amen

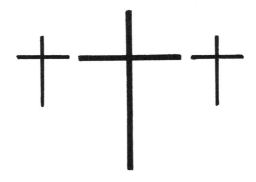

29 – Set of three crosses

Handout 13
Big Cross, Little Crosses

Before every service a deacon would pray, 'Dear Lord, as we enter into your house, take away all thoughts of the world.' A devout woman, loving and caring in her daily life, her prayer reflects a pious other-worldly understanding of Christianity.

The Jesuit Indian priest, Anthony de Mello, has a similar story about a very religious woman who attended church daily. En route, children would call to her, neighbours greeted her, beggars accosted her, but she was so immersed in her devotions that she was oblivious to them all. Great was her distress when one day she couldn't get the church door to open, however hard she pushed. She eventually realized that it was locked and that she would miss Mass for the first time ever. Then, right in front of her, she found a note pinned to the door. It said, 'I'm out there!'[1] For such people the Church represents a spiritual realm, with the real world being regarded as outside the scope of God's reign. In following an other-worldly Jesus, they are in the world but not of it.

At Calvary, the cross of Christ is flanked by two crosses on which two common men died a painful death along with Jesus. These men represent you and me. Not only do they stand for the sinful human race but they remind us of the personal crosses that we all bear in our daily lives. The Church, in its liturgy and theology, routinely stresses the big, cosmic cross of Jesus, but seldom invites us to reflect on the little crosses that each one of us carries. If we dwell only on the cross of Jesus, then we risk losing sight of our own suffering, the Calvary in our lives as well as in the lives of our families, communities and nations, which God came in Christ to heal. Our heavenly Father offers the supreme sacrifice as a direct response to our suffering. Hence, any understanding of the cross which fails to relate it to our existential situation misses its real significance.

In recent times, liberation theologians in Latin America have tried to remedy this error by taking account of the socio-economic and political injustices in their continent, connecting the many little crosses of their people to the cross of Jesus. As Gustavo Gutiérrez, a Roman Catholic priest, observes from within the shanty towns in Peru,

> If I lived complacently with three meals a day, a siesta, and a secure life, untouched by what is going on around me, then climb into the pulpit on Sunday and tell the people 'God loves you', what I say will sound hollow, like a clanging cymbal. The challenge of the gospel is its power to transform me and my attitudes and my whole way of life, so that my words will be truly meaningful to those to whom I proclaim it. It is good news only if it makes sense to them in their concrete lives.[2]

This genuinely incarnational theology of the cross is firmly rooted in a specific context, linking the suffering of a particular people in a particular place with the cross of Jesus. That is why it is so relevant in our Christian witness today and has spawned so many related theologies like Black theology in Africa, Dalit theology in India, Water Buffalo theology in Thailand, and a global feminist theology.

Our Personal Little Crosses of Pain and Suffering

However, although Latin American liberation theology moved us on in incorporating the socio-political dimensions of the cross, it downplayed the personal dimension of our existential pain. Our link with the big cross of Jesus was thus limited to the tribal crosses of communities and nations. But Christian salvation is as much personal as it is communal. As members of the Body of Christ we naturally share in the transformation of our respective communities. But in addition, we have a personal relationship with Jesus, manifesting itself in silence, prayer and contemplation. Here we begin to link the cross of Jesus with the little crosses of the people of God.

In the words of Meister Eckhart, a medieval German mystic, 'What good is it that Christ died at Calvary and rose again from the holy tomb if Christ did not die also within me and did not rise again within me?' The big cross remains a remote concept unless we become aware of how our personal pain is related to the pain of God. Once we have made that connection, we are equally sure of sharing in the little resurrection which is the promise of the gospel of Christ.

Time is allowed for reflection on Handout No. 13.

Bible Study No. 1

'For in him all the fullness of God was pleased to dwell, and through him God was pleased to reconcile to himself all things, whether on earth or in heaven, by making peace through the blood of his cross' (Colossians 1.19–20).

- Reflect on how some of the little crosses in your life relate to the big cross of Jesus. Make a list of these little crosses. If appropriate, this can be shared with someone else.
- God sets us free by making 'peace through the blood of Jesus' cross'. How do we experience this liberation in our lives?

Time is allowed for reflection followed by sharing in pairs if desired, otherwise continue with silent meditation.

Notes

1 Anthony de Mello, 1988, *Taking Flight: A Book of Story Meditations*, New York, London: Image Books, Doubleday, pp. 33–4.
2 Cited in 'Christian tasks in contemporary Japan', *Japan Christian Quarterly*, Spring 1990, pp. 93–7.

5

GOOD FRIDAY PILGRIM STORIES

Programme for a Half-Day Event or the Other Half of the First Session

	Refreshments at the start or lunch break.
1 hour:	Selected stories as short talks, or else given as handouts for reflection.
30 minutes:	Bible study No. 2 – possible sharing in pairs.
15 minutes:	Tea break.
1 hour:	Focus on the story of Sudanese Christians – Handout 17 or on 'Healing the Wounded, Crucified Earth' – Handout 18 for reflection or working in pairs and possible discussion on things to do.
30 minutes:	Closing Worship: 'Liturgy for the Dispossessed' or one of the Creation Liturgies as cited.

Good Friday Pilgrims

Good Friday is thought to be derived from 'God's Friday'. It was known as 'Holy or Great Friday' in Romance languages, 'Sorrowful Friday' in German, and 'Long Friday' by the Anglo-Saxons because of the long fast endured that day. For early Christians every Friday was a feast day so that the Friday before Easter, commemorating Christ's crucifixion, became the holiest of days. Over time, the day was dedicated to fasting, penance and prayer. Before Bank Holidays were introduced in England, Good Friday and Christmas Day were the only days off for workers.

We see Good Friday pilgrims as those people who have been transformed by a crucifying experience, or whose witness embodies the carrying of a little cross either for themselves or their community. God's unconditional loving solidarity in sharing in our suffering reveals the power of the cross, enabling believers to challenge and even change a crucified situation. Their stories are used in meditation and in workshops so that we may reflect more deeply on what it means to live the cross.

(The facilitator needs to select those stories that are relevant to a specific event, be it worship, a retreat, a Quiet Day, or a weekend away for a group; and would fit in with a chosen theme. All the stories are available as handouts.)

Handout 14
Being Transformed by a Crucifying Event

Story no. 1: A French Roman Catholic Archbishop as a Young Man

30 – Three African crosses

The Archbishop tells of how, some years back, a group of bored teenage boys gathered on the Cathedral Square in Paris looking for trouble. They had the idea of compiling a list of the most horrible sins imaginable and then shocking the old priest on duty in the cathedral with their bogus confession. They drew lots, with one poor lad having to brave the confessional with this sorry tale. Much to his surprise, the old priest remained unmoved, but only quietly said, 'Before I proclaim absolution, I want you to go over to that large crucifix, kneel down and look straight into the eyes of Jesus Christ as you say these words: "Jesus, I know you died for me, but I don't care a damn!" Then come back and we'll talk.' The story ends there, but there is no doubting its veracity because the Archbishop was that same young man.

Story no. 2: Abraham Lieta, Anglican Priest in Lesotho

As a boy, Abraham attended a Roman Catholic mission school. His lasting memory is of a German nun who was overly enthusiastic in meting out punishment with a ruler. Abraham recalls her giving a graphic account of the Crucifixion, dwelling on all the most gruesome details. The children were awestruck, and even more puzzled when she concluded by saying, 'and still we continue to crucify Christ today'.

Taking courage, Abraham challenged her, arguing that Christ's crucifixion was past history. Frozen in terror he waited for the dreaded ruler to come crashing down. Instead, in shocked silence, the nun asked the class to pray for him that he might gain a deeper understanding of Christ's Passion and its continued relevance in their lives. Abraham was far more mortified by his classmates' prayers than any corporal chastisement. Yet this was a turning point in his life. In coming to realize the awful truth that we do indeed permit Christ to be crucified again and again in all the suffering in the world today, he decided to offer himself for ordination, following in the footsteps of his father and grandfather.

Story no. 3: John, a Priest in England

John was the newly appointed Anglican priest in a former mining community in County Durham. Having attended a Catholic school, he still felt the shame of a carpentry class in which an angry monk had thrown his ham-fisted efforts to make a cross for his mother into a waste-paper basket, sending him home empty handed. As the incumbent of his first parish, he bravely decided to help his church's fundraising efforts by making crosses for sale. With the help of the churchwarden he triumphed. When his wife heard the story for the first time, she went straight into the garden and made a small crown of thorns to encircle each cross.

Bible Study No. 2

'But God proves his love for us in that while we still were sinners Christ died for us' (Romans 5.8).

- How do we still crucify Christ today? Examples can be written down, and shared with a partner if so wished.
- To what extent do marginalized people look to your church to engage with their needs and aspirations? How could you come alongside in helping them to help themselves? What action is needed?

Handout 15
The Cross as a Symbol of Non-Violent Resistance in South Africa

Story no. 4: Prophetic Witness of Clergy

During the liberation struggle in South Africa, the ever more draconian laws made public protest illegal. With the black townships going up in flames and the youth being mercilessly hunted down and imprisoned, the Church was finally forced to move from its cautious criticism of apartheid to becoming actively involved in non-violent civil disobedience. One of the most significant peace initiatives took place in 1988 when leaders of different denominations held a service in St George's Cathedral, Cape Town, before taking a petition to the Houses of Parliament nearby. With arms linked, ranks of robed clergy processed into the street to be met by a phalanx of heavily armed police. The clergy responded by kneeling down on the pavement to pray and refused to budge. The world's media had a field day photographing eminent church leaders being bundled into police vans while water cannons were used to disperse the congregation. More importantly, the cross had now become a widely accepted symbol of non-violent resistance.

Story no. 5: Archbishop Tutu as the Rabble-Rouser for Peace

Archbishop Tutu, fondly known as the rabble-rouser for peace, was often seen carrying a large wooden cross and leading crowds of people in protest at the escalating violence of the apartheid regime. His trouble-making earned him a Nobel Peace Prize, while the people rejoiced that the Church had at last become involved in prophetic action.[1]

Prayer of Archbishop Desmond Tutu

Goodness is stronger than evil;
Love is stronger than hate;
Light is stronger than darkness;
Life is stronger than death;
Victory is ours through Him who loves us.

Story no. 6: Good Friday in Durban: Peace through the Cross

One Good Friday over 3,000 people processed through the streets of Durban, each person holding up a small wooden cross on which was written, 'Peace through the cross'. Beginning with the singing of *Nkosi Sikilel' iAfrika*, 'God Bless Africa', they marched across the city to the continuous tolling of church bells. It was a time of intense violence in 'the killing fields of Natal' and the large cross carried up front had been made from the blackened timbers of the burnt-out house of a Roman Catholic woman. An armed faction had wanted to kill her children, but failing to find them decided to kill her instead. When she insisted on donning her Mothers' Union uniform first, they were shamed into saying that they 'couldn't kill their mother', but they torched her house. After the march had ended, the cross was planted on the border between the warring factions. It came to symbolize a cross of life as people pinned flowers and greenery on it for many weeks afterwards.

31 – Peace cross

Story no. 7: The Young and the Old

The barbed wire crucifix made by Roman Catholic youth in South Africa is another evocative symbol of this troubled time. Rolls of barbed wire surrounded their townships, an ever-present symbol of military constraint and impending violence. Yet for these youngsters, Christ was not only with them in their situation but was a liberating figure, transcending time and space and offering hope in their darkest hours.

A small ebony cross made by an old woman in a remote resettlement camp in the north speaks of a different kind of suffering. Not only is ebony an extremely hard wood, which must have taken hours to carve with makeshift implements, but the woman was so poor that she couldn't even afford a thong on which to thread her cross. Instead, she made use of a thin strip of rubber, roughly shredded from an old car tyre. For this she received a mere pittance.

32 – Barbed Wire Crucifix

Handout 16
Carrying the Cross for One's Community

Story no. 8: Latin American Martyrs

In Latin America, the Maria Christina Gomez cross from El Salvador is a memorial to yet more oppression and violence in our time. Brightly painted on wood, the cross celebrates the life and faith of a young Baptist teacher who was kidnapped and killed because of her involvement with a base Christian community, working according to gospel values for social and political change.[2] Similarly, a crucifix, richly decorated with indigenous imagery, commemorates the murder of six Jesuit monks and a lay couple in San Salvador in 1989. The text used, 'Blessed are those who are persecuted in the cause of right; theirs is the Kingdom of Heaven' (Matthew 5.10), applies to many Good Friday pilgrims, as with the next story.

Story no. 9: Witnessing as a Persecuted Christian Minority in a Muslim Country

At a human rights conference in Oxford, a Malaysian Methodist minister explained that in belonging to a persecuted minority in a Muslim country, Christians had three options: shut up, pack up (and go), or take up (the cross). 'In prison our life becomes the last weapon the authorities can use against us,' he said. 'We compromise if we give in so as to carry on living. But if we say, "Blessed are those who die in the Lord, you can take my life and do with it as you will", then they have lost their last weapon. That is where freedom lies because then we live out Christ. We must commit ourselves and our churches to Christ even to surrendering our lives if we are to be totally faithful. Please pray for us.'[3]

Story no. 10: Prophetic Action by Filipino Women

In the Philippines, a unique form of prophetic action enabled the Kalingo-Apayo women to save their precious land from the building of a dam. These mountain people are mostly Roman Catholic, as is the rest of their country. Such is their identification with Christ's Passion that one will say to the other, 'Move over, it is my turn on the cross.' Over the years they had managed to repulse successive waves of colonial invaders, until they were threatened with the building of the Chico River Dam, a joint enterprise of government and multi-national funding. The dam would have flooded the valley where they lived, not only displacing thousands of people but submerging their villages and farmland, with their only source of sustenance and traditional way of living being obliterated.

When the construction workers started unloading equipment at the dam site, the women loaded it all back again. When the wall started to take shape, the women razed it to the ground overnight. Ultimately, the military were summoned. On arrival, the troops were met by hundreds of women who at a given signal stripped off their blouses and confronted them with bare breasts. The troops scattered in confusion. Undaunted by threats of arrest, the women set up camp with their cooking pots, children, dogs and chickens next to the military compound and used it as a rubbish dump. The soldiers finally sued for peace and the Chico River Dam was never built.

Handout 17
Christian Witness in the Sudan

Story no. 11: 'Forever Stuck to the Cross'

The late Marc Nikkel, who served the Episcopal Church in Sudan during the 1990s, made a study of the cross among the Nilotic Bor Dinka Christians in Southern Sudan, more especially the long-shafted processional crosses of which he had a substantial collection.[4] His work provides a contemporary example of true images of the cross which relate to a time of devastating social upheaval and suffering during a civil war.

Uprooted by the onslaught of the Nationalist Islamic Front, tens of thousands of Dinka were dispersed in refugee camps, many fleeing across the border into the northern Kenyan desert. The processional crosses, crafted of local woods and scrap metal, and decorated with anything from ivory and cow-horns to brass bullet

33 – Sudanese mud cross

casings and white plastic, tell a story of faith and courage, of the will to survive amidst displacement, famine and disease. One ebony cross was topped with the spiralled head of a rocket-propelled grenade (RPG), while its base consisted of a large-gauge, brass bullet shell. These were picked up by evangelist James Lual Achol in a battle zone. As he explained the meaning of his cross to Nikkel,

> Jesus brought the good news but was crucified with the spikes that nailed him down. In the same way, the gospel has come to our land in Southern Sudan, and we suffer for his word, that which we accepted. Our children are made into slaves because of it. We are put to death because of it. Our cattle have all been raided because of it. All those who receive the gospel will suffer, and so do we. In this day the RPG is used as a tool of killing against our people as certainly as spikes were used to crucify Jesus on the cross. Still, we carry within us the hope that we will ultimately have victory through the cross of Christ. It is the cross that will judge between us and the aggressors who seek to kill us. I want people in the West to see the cross brought to them from Sudan because it is the cross they once brought to us. I want them to see that we are people like them and this is the suffering it has brought us. We have given up our old divinities, and virtually everything we possess, and we have taken up the cross alone. Pray for us that we will remain crucified upon the cross, that we will remain faithful. We are forever stuck to the cross.

What is remarkable is that these people resisted the best efforts of CMS missionaries for eight decades. It was only as a result of the carnage of war and widespread displacement from ancestral lands, when their old way of life was torn apart and the powers of traditional divinities were no longer effective, that the gospel took root and spread with unprecedented speed. An indigenous leadership, employing vernacular idioms and thousands of newly composed songs, has been at the forefront of incarnating the teachings and symbols of Christianity within the traditional thought-patterns and values of the Dinka culture. This exemplary form of inculturation focused on the cross has provided continuity with the past while meeting new religious and social needs.

Amidst the ravages of war, the Bor Dinka crosses proclaim that God, *Nhialic*, is ever present among his people. Endowed with authority to supplant every form of evil, the cross derives its power from an intimate identification with Christ and his sacrificial death. As Nikkel observes,

> For many Dinka Christians the cross embodies Christ, and Christ embodies the cross. Amidst the insecurity of war and destitution, it is a tangible representation

of his presence as sacrificial Lamb, Kinsman, Parent, Reconciler and Redeemer. The multi-faceted symbol they raise aloft reflects his atoning, healing and nurturing presence.[5]

Crosses are found on trees and decorated calabashes, stitched into vestments and banners, on the garments of Mothers' Union and choir members, worn as decorations in girls' hair and around the necks of young and old, carved into plastic or ivory as wrist or arm bands, and gracing the handlebars of pastors' bicycles. Bundles of woven grasses form crosses to crown the roofs of churches, private huts and cattle byres of believers, while mud churches are constructed on cruciform floor plans.

However, it is the long-shafted crosses carried by most Bor Dinka Christians which are the most striking. Among these semi-nomadic people, their usage has evolved from the traditional role of sticks and spears for men – as walking-sticks, for ritual usage or prestige, as potential weapons, or for fishing and hunting. Although the crosses may still function as staffs, they are now radically transformed to encompass a whole new range of religious meanings and functions, with women using them most for healing rituals, exorcisms and Christian witness. The most amazing sight is to see thousands of believers thrusting a forest of crosses heavenward with every beat of their songs, whether they are marching to greet their bishop or in procession on a holy day. It is the crucified and risen Christ whose cross these Christian warriors bear, as they march into spiritual battle against the many forces of evil.

Things To Do Relating to Good Friday Pilgrims

- On a Quiet Day or in a workshop, stories can be shared about people you either know, have read about, or seen on television, who could be regarded as Good Friday pilgrims.
- Support partnership links with suffering communities around the world, receiving as well as giving in whatever way seems possible.

Handout 18
Healing of the Crucified, Wounded Earth

Story no. 12: A Compassionate Ministry in South Africa

In South Africa, Canon Morriat Nceba Gabula has followed a different path as a Good Friday pilgrim, concentrating on healing the crucified, wounded earth as a way of providing his people with a means of survival while giving them back their humanity. Morriat lives between the Drakensberg mountains and the Indian Ocean in what was northern Transkei. This was a dumping ground for the forced removal of Xhosa people during the apartheid era. With unemployment reaching 75 per cent, overpopulation and over-grazing have made it one of the most environmentally degraded areas in the country.

Morriat's concern for creation began during his mission-school days, winning prizes for the best garden plot, and continued with vegetable growing during his ordination training. His vision of 'evangelism with a spade' was inspired by a visiting speaker who asked how they could preach to people with hungry stomachs. Morriat believes that the Church has waited far too long to start development work, God having initiated it in the Garden of Eden with Adam. For him, 'This was the first sustainable agriculture! Our mission, to go back to creation, is a call to liberate the people of our region.'[6] In 1999, his bishop released him to follow 'the compassionate ministry of Christ' as a full-time development worker. All Morriat asked for was a cross, a Bible and a spade.

Without a budget, he used his small stipend to grow potatoes at his homestead in Lusikisiki. With the money made from selling his first crop, he started teaching people around the diocese to care for their eroded earth with fencing, water conservation and soil reclamation. The locals in turn bought his seed potatoes, enabling them to grow food for their families and to sell the surplus. Morriat went on to plant fruit trees, initiate a heifer project, start a pre-school, and share his expertise in diocesan projects. Happily, the newly formed Diocese of Umzimvubu embarked on a 'Back to Eden' project: a sustainable agricultural and environmental education programme to assist the poor in their rural communities. By improving their land use practices they became self-supporting while healing the earth and regaining their dignity as people.

When children come to be baptized, Morriat waives the fee, asking only that parents plant a fruit tree in the name of the child. As the tree grows, so will the child until he can care for it himself. Eventually it will bear fruit, giving the youngster a balanced diet and providing income towards his education. An engaged spirituality centred on the cross has sustained Morriat's unique mission 'to mobilize families to be aware of God's creation around them, and celebrate life in all its fullness'.

Morriat's Prayer

Lord God of our ancestors, from whom we have inherited this earth with all its beauty and richness, forgive us for destroying your creation. The land lies bare and desolate, full of crevices and gullies. Animals have been killed by ravaging fires. There are no more gushing springs or singing birds in dense forests, no more beautiful flora and vegetation. Oh God, we are so sorry we have nothing to hand over to our children. We humbly request your forgiveness and pardon for our ignorance and negligence.

We praise and thank you, Heavenly Father, for the beauty and bounty of your creation. Open our minds to the gifts you have given us with which we may heal your wounded earth, for the love of your son, Jesus Christ, our crucified and risen Lord. Amen.

Story no. 13: Healing the Wounded Earth in Britain

34 – Sea pinks and crosses

In Britain, a Garden of Remembrance set among bleak rows of former colliery houses near Gateshead provides an imaginative example of the healing of our wounded earth. The austere red-brick church of Dunston St Nicholas was built in 1965, but the grounds remained a derelict wasteland, littered with broken glass and rubbish. After many years, the parish decided to turn their churchyard into a rose garden, each bush commemorating someone in their community. Together with a winter jasmine-covered fence, a honeysuckle arch, a water feature and seats, the garden has become 'a haven of peace and tranquillity', attracting many regular visitors. Moreover, with the continued planting of memorial roses it has become an ideal setting for wedding photographs, leading to a marked increase in church weddings. People are drawn to the foot of the cross in many different ways.

In trying to live out the meaning of the cross, these stories of Good Friday pilgrims and the healing of God's wounded earth are given to inspire us. In addition, Weber has brought together thought-provoking reflections with pictures of crosses from around the world in *On a Friday Noon: Meditations Under the Cross*.

Things To Do in Healing Our Earth

1 What can your church do to practise best stewardship of its land, buildings, energy use, recycling, support for Fair Trade, etc.?
2 How could your church seek to support rural communities – through prayer, buying their produce, establishing rural–urban church links, involving young people in ecological concerns, etc.?
3 An ecumenical Earthcare Group could be formed to act as an advisory body to local faith communities on conservation, effective use of energy, recycling, 'green' funerals, campaigning, becoming eco-congregations, theological and liturgical resourcing, etc.

Closing Worship: Liturgy for the Dispossessed

Appropriate hymns, songs and choruses may be sung at any point during worship, or music played.

Leader The Lord who heard the cry of his people be with you.
All Alleluia. The Lord is merciful indeed. (Exodus 3.7–9)

Call to worship

Leader Lord Jesus, we are gathered in worship; remind us of the lowly manger, the lonely cross and the empty tomb. For these are powerful symbols of a life offered to establish a new creation, where weeping and crying for help will be no more, where people no longer die in infancy, where peasants plant and enjoy the fruits of their labour, where workers build houses and inhabit them, where evil powers no longer reign supreme. Create in us, O Lord, this kind of life. Amen. (Philippines)[7]

Psalm 91 The Lord is my refuge.
Suggested reading Luke 6.20–26.

Meditation

'One Person's Dream is Another's Nightmare', or use one or two of the stories given above.

The dream of the mighty for more power, of the rich for more wealth, is the nightmare of the powerless and the poor. But the dream of the oppressed and the poor for liberation is the nightmare of the powerful and the rich. It has always been so in a world which is unwilling to share resources and to discern them as gifts, not possessions.

The dream of the oppressed is utopian, it is a vision of a better world. It is this vision which enabled the first Christians to face persecution. 'Then I saw a new heaven and a new earth.' It is the same vision which has motivated the prophets throughout the centuries, the vision of the Kingdom of God inaugurated in Jesus Christ but yet to come in its fullness. This vision threatens those who possess everything except the ability to share with others. The powerful and privileged fear the dreams of the poor and the visions of the prophets because they derive from the coming of the Kingdom of God, God's purpose for his world. They are dreams and visions which are just and right, and will come true. (South Africa)[8]

A time of silent reflection

Leader   Listen to the cries of the tillers of the soil, their songs of
freedom, their shouts for justice, their prayers for peace. In responding concretely to those in need we would truly experience the blessings of God. Amen. (Philippines)[9]

Prayer from the Christian Conference of Asia

All   Give us, O Lord, churches,
that will be more courageous than cautious;
that will not merely 'comfort the afflicted' but 'afflict the comfortable';

that will not only love the world but will also judge the world;

that will not only pursue peace but also demand justice;

that will not remain silent when people are calling for a voice;

that will not pass by on the other side when wounded humanity is
waiting to be healed;

that will follow Christ even when the way points to the cross.

To this end we offer ourselves in the name of him who loved us and gave
himself for us. Amen. (Author unknown)

Benediction

Leader   May the blessing of God Almighty who became poor in Christ, empower
us all to overcome the world.

All   Amen. We shall overcome. Alleluia. (Philippians 2.5–8; John 16.33)

Liturgies on Creation

'Deep Peace of the Quiet Earth. Celtic reflections on the integrity of creation'
in *Let All the World: Liturgies, Litanies and Prayers from Around the World*,
1990, London: USPG, SPCK, pp. 75–86 (with songs).

'A Celtic Liturgy in the Tradition of the Carmina Gadelica' (Order of Service for
Holy Communion), pp. 17–24, and 'For the Healing of the Nations: An Order
of Service to Celebrate Creation' in Kate Wyles (ed.), *From Shore to Shore*,
2003, London: USPG.

'When the Time was Right' (creation story), pp. 55–7, and 'On the Eighth Day' (the
undoing of creation), pp. 58–63 in John Bell, *He Was in the World: Meditations
for Public Worship*, 1995, Glasgow: Wild Goose Publications.

Notes

1 John Allen, 2006, *Rabble-Rouser for Peace: The Authorised Biography of Desmond
Tutu*, London: Rider, Ebury Publishing.

2 Image no. 3 in *The Christ We Share* pack, 2nd edn, 2000, London: USPG, Methodist
Church, CMS.

3 Revd Daniel Ho, the National Evangelical Fellowship of Malaysia, 1992.

4 This section is based on the work of Marc Nikkel, with personal interviews in Edinburgh
during the 1990s; CMS Link Letters from Nairobi, 30 May 1995 and 12 February 1997;
and the initial draft of 'The Cross of Bor Dinka Christians as Flag, Weapon and Memorial
to Sacrifice', used with the permission of the late author. Nikkel was jointly appointed by the
Church Mission Society, Episcopal Church USA and the Diocese of Southwestern Virginia,
USA.

5 Nikkel, 'The Cross', p. 10.

6 This story is based on personal communications in 2006 and 2009. In 2001, Fr Morriat was made 'Community Builder of the Year' by the Eastern Cape Government.

7 Bartolome Espartero, 1993, 'Liturgy for Advent', in *USPG: Anglicans in World Mission, Transmission*. Fr Bart is from the Philippine Independent Church, linked to the Anglican Communion.

8 John De Gruchy, 1986, 'One Person's Dream is Another's Nightmare', in *Cry Justice: Prayers, Meditations and Readings from South Africa*, London: Collins, pp. 232–3.

9 Espartero, *USPG Transmission*.

PART 3
WORKING WITH CROSSES

35 – AIDS service

*36 – South African child looking
at a cross*

37 – 'Raped'

6

WORKSHOPS WITH CROSSES

Programme for a Weekend Event (suggested timing only)

Parts of the programme can be used either for a half-day or full day event, as with a Quiet Day, or dipped into over a longer period as in a retreat. The pick-and-mix selection of modules is then advised, including exercises at the end of the chapter.

Friday Evening

20 minutes: Welcome, presentation of the programme, practical arrangements, introductions.

10 minutes: Opening Worship.

5 minutes: Short talk – 'Early History of Crosses' (Ch. 1).

c. 45 minutes: Presentation of some images of the cross on the CD-ROM – time given for reflection.
  Denominational Evening Prayers/Compline if wished.

Opening Worship

'May I never boast of anything except the cross of our Lord Jesus Christ, by which the world has been crucified to me, and I to the world' (Galatians 6.14).

Leader   Were you there when they made the cross of Jesus?

All   Did you touch the cross on which our Saviour hung?

Leader   The cross stands tall on the hill of Calvary.

All	Yes, the cross that we witness throughout the world.
Leader	Let us all gather around the cross of Jesus
All	and view it from many angles and sides.
Leader	Let us meditate on the cross of Jesus
All	in the shape that is dearest to our hearts.
Leader	One cross, one Saviour, one salvation
All	in the diversity of our prayers to the Lord. Amen.

This is followed by a short time of quiet reflection and prayer.

Saturday Morning – Programme (with options)

Note to facilitator: in a workshop participants are seated either in one big circle or in a few smaller ones depending on numbers. A relaxed atmosphere with comfortable seating and temperature helps to create the right mood. In a church, moveable chairs are better than pews. A display of crosses is set out beforehand on tables, visible to all and with as wide a selection as possible.

Saturday Morning Programme

	Denominational Morning Worship (optional)
5 minutes:	Short introductory talk on crosses
35 minutes:	Session 1: Talk on basic forms of crosses and crucifixes – handout 1 (see page 15) illustrated where possible.
5 minutes:	Short break.
45 minutes:	Session 2: Talk on 'True Images of the Cross' with stories of saints and their crosses (see page 27) and actual crosses if available, and handouts.
	Or talk on 'Big, Cross, Little Crosses' and some stories of Good Friday pilgrims (Part 2, Chs 4 and 5), with handouts. Time allowed for reflection.
30 minutes:	Tea break.
c. 1 hour:	Session 3: Workshop with crosses.
	Option 1: using a display of crosses.
	Option 2: using people's own crosses.
30 minutes:	Holy Eucharist or Denominational Worship (optional). Negotiate time for lunch break and rest period

Handout 19
Introductory Talk on Crosses

The place of the cross, whether in personal devotions or organized worship, is unique. Unlike anything else liturgically, it reminds us of a concrete event in our salvation history. The cross is three-dimensional so that it can be approached from any vantage point. It can be touched, allowing one to make contact with the profound truth it symbolizes, while its hard reality excludes any idea of the poetic or romantic. It can be held, giving a sense of intimate nearness to the loving God whom it proclaims. It can be raised up high so as to lift up one's faith in the risen Christ. It can be kissed, showing a person's deep love for the Incarnation, or knelt in front of in veneration for what it represents.

All these different facets can be included in working with crosses; but we use them as a way of enabling people to explore, nurture, and share their faith so as to further the mission of God, *missio Dei*. Working with images of Christ has a similar purpose;[1] but whereas pictures are one-dimensional, crosses are tactile and can evoke a deeper response. They also provide a more creative engagement through artistry, crafts, and liturgy.

For some people holding or handling a cross may be a new experience and time should be given to working through any feelings this may evoke.

Session 1: Talk on Basic Forms of the Cross (see page 15).

Session 2: Talk on 'True Images of the Cross' or on 'Big Cross, Little Crosses', with Stories and Handouts (see Chs 3 and 4).

Session 3: Workshop with Crosses (Handout no. 19 for both options.)

Option 1: Working with a display of crosses

Choose a cross from the display, followed by a time of **silent reflection**. Questions are given as a focus for meditation, their choice depending on the nature of the event, as is the time taken for reflection.

On a Quiet Day or Retreat these questions could take up most of a day.

Questions for Reflection and Discussion:

- Why did you choose this cross?
- What meaning does the cross have in your life?
- Can you identify with the person who made your cross, or the context or country from which it comes?
- What has influenced you in choosing either a cross or a crucifix from the display?
- In what way does your chosen cross reflect the little crosses you carry in your daily life? How does it relate to the big cross of Jesus?

Sharing: After a time of reflection you may wish to share in pairs.

If a number of questions are to be addressed the discussion can be broken up into shorter time slots with an optional change of partner. The discussion should be open-ended giving people space to explore their ideas and feelings. There are no right or wrong answers.

Option 2: Working with your own crosses

Participants are asked to bring their own or borrowed crosses. Using the same format as given above, a time of **silent reflection** may be followed by **sharing**. However, because of the personal nature of many of the crosses this may well be an emotional experience for some, and they should be free to share only as much as feels comfortable to them.

Questions for Discussion:

- What is the story of your cross? – an heirloom, a confirmation gift, found during travels or on a pilgrimage, a present to mark a special occasion, linked to a close friend, family member or pastor, etc.
- What has your cross meant to you on your spiritual journey? If borrowed, what does it mean to you now?
- What does the wearing of a cross mean to you?
- In what way does this cross represent the little crosses you carry in your daily life? How does it relate to the big cross of Jesus?

Plenary Session for Both Sessions

The small groups are reconvened. Members then take turns in sharing what the cross they have chosen or brought with them means to them, and how they responded to different questions. No one needs to say more than they wish. In a final plenary session participants can be invited to reflect on their experience and to ask any outstanding questions.

Saturday Afternoon and Evening Programme

1½ hours	Session 4: Making your own crosses or collages.
30 minutes	Tea break.
c. 1 hour	Session 5: Share what your cross or collage means to you.
	Mount a display – optional.
	Supper.
1 hour	Session 6:
	Option 1: Reflect on more images of the cross on CD-ROM.
	Option 2: Talk or reflection on more stories from chapters 3 (True Images of the Cross) or 5 (Good Friday Pilgrim Stories).
End of Day	Denominational Evening Prayers/Compline or
	Closing Worship (if time is limited to one day).

27 – Maltese cross

Session 4: Making Your Own Crosses or Collages

Resources needed: A few tables are needed to set out a selection of resources – a hammer, pliers, nails in different sizes, off-cuts of wood, string, wire (copper electrical wire is popular), pipe cleaners, raffia, pieces of material, paper towel rolls, medical tongue depressors, crayons, felt tip pens, paints, A1 paper, newspapers and magazines, a good number of scissors, glue, coloured drawing pins, needles, tapestry wools, plastic embroidery canvas, etc. In a garden setting, twigs, leaves, flowers and stones may be used, while in an urban context carefully selected rubbish is another option.

Crosses: Participants are given complete freedom in making their cross.

Collages may involve a number of participants and are ideal with an all-age group, for those needing moral support, or with younger people. Suitable pictures, words and headlines are cut out of newspapers and magazines, and can be pasted in abstract designs or else around the central motif of a cross. Drawings are equally applicable. A particular theme can be followed such as violence, substance abuse, homelessness, children, the elderly, families, justice and creation, global warming, or the destruction of the environment. Otherwise, the focus could be on a particular country, or on the latest news (good and bad) of what is happening in the world. Additional information, scriptural texts, or phrases such as 'Lord, give us the strength to follow the way of the cross', can be written in.

Session 5: Share What Your Cross or Collage Means to You

Participants are invited to share what their cross or collage is about:

- What inspired you in making your cross or collage?
- What are you trying to communicate about the cross?
- What has this exercise meant to you?

Participants should take their crosses and collages home with them. Mounting a display in church is a way of extending the experience so that others may share in it, but anonymity is advised.

Session 6

Option 1: Reflect on more images of the cross on CD-ROM.
Option 2: Talk or Reflection on more stories from Chapter 3 (True Images of the Cross) or Chapter 5 (Good Friday Pilgrim Stories).

If time is limited to one day then the following **Closing Worship** can be used at the end of the afternoon.

Closing Worship

Introductory Sentence 'And I, when I am lifted up from the earth, will draw all people to myself.' (John 12.32)

Collect for Holy Cross Day (14 September)

Almighty God, in the passion of your blessed Son
you made an instrument of shameful death
to be for us the means of life;
grant us so to glory in the Cross of Christ
that we may gladly suffer for his sake,
who lives and reigns with you and the Holy Spirit,
one God now and for ever. Amen. (New Zealand)[2]

Psalm 98: 'O sing to the Lord a new song'
Suggested Readings: Isaiah 45.20–25; Philippians 2.5–11; John 12.31–36a

Meditation
The Message of the Cross in Africa

'The central message of the earliest community of believers was "Christ nailed to the cross" (1 Corinthians 1.23; 2.2). The cross was the heart of the gospel and many in the history of the church were to experience crucifixion and other types of persecution . . . Many have come to experience and know the cross; many have come to know the meaning of the cross through other experience. Can it be a surprise that the cross was at the heart of the gospel? Can it be a surprise that it is the poor, those who suffer and those who are marginalized, who have welcomed in a deeper way the word of the cross? Africans came to know the cross in their situation of misery. We have come to see the cross of Jesus Christ as the cross of the South, thus carrying within ourselves the hidden Christ.' (Ghana)[3]

Collect for Holy Cross Day

Jesus, crucified and risen,
you have turned a criminal's cross
into release and reconciliation.
Let us who are marked with the cross
be not ashamed to witness to you.
Amen. (New Zealand)[4]

Ritual Acts During Worship

Various ritual acts can be carried out during the liturgy to enhance the worship experience.

- A basket full of river stones or pebbles, washed clean, are used to represent our individual burdens. After taking a stone, participants spend time in silence reflecting on what burden it represents to them. They then come forward to place their stone at the foot of a cross.
- Similarly, people can write down their burdens, petitions or confessions on pieces of paper and leave them in a basket next to the cross. These can be prayed over later.

Other suitable liturgies include 'The Litany of the Cross' in *Patterns for Worship*,[5] or the readings and prayers for Holy Cross Day (14 September) in the Church of England *ASB 1980*.[6]

Sunday Morning Programme

	Denominational Worship (optional).
2 hours:	Session 7: Liturgy workshop focusing on the Cross and preparing for worship.
30 minutes:	Tea break.
c. 1 hour:	Session 8: Cross liturgy as devised by participants.
	Lunch and Farewells.

Session 7: Liturgy Workshop

Background Information: Continuing with the theme of the cross, jobs are allocated to prepare for worship. This should include a welcome, confession (and absolution if desired), selection of Bible readings, composition or selection of prayers, co-ordination of sharing the peace, arranging the setting, someone to give a short homily or else a dramatic group presentation. A small choir is needed to select songs and hymns, and to lead the singing. If musicians are not available, recorded music can be used. If there is to be a Eucharist, an ordained person will need to make appropriate preparations, but an *agape* feast would be just as relevant. Working in small groups gives confidence to the less assured, with any ministers present taking a back seat (or quietly disappearing!).

Resources should include Bibles, a range of liturgical material, books of prayers, musical instruments, a CD player, and songs and hymns with music. One way of identifying with Christians in other parts of the world is to learn their songs. John Bell from the Iona Community has published songbooks with tape-recorded music, and singalongs work well.[7]

Division of Tasks

- **A good co-ordinator** is needed to ensure continuity: to check that a master plan of the liturgy is drawn up and copied, that the groups are clear about their respective roles and when to contribute their input, that everyone is involved, and that the liturgy will flow smoothly.
- **The music group** is responsible for seeing that the words of songs and hymns are available either in print or on an overhead projector. They need to consult with the other groups to make a relevant selection. Prayers can be greatly enhanced by soft background music, recorded or live. So too, if a drama group is to present the ministry of the word, they may have musical requirements.
- **The prayer group** can also include a short affirmation of faith in their slot. Ideally, at least some prayers are composed by participants; however, using prayers from the World Church could introduce a new dimension into regular worship.
- **A drama group** can act out a selected Bible reading, or else someone can be delegated to give a **short homily** (could be the minister).
- **An organizing group** will be delegated to arrange the seating. Using the shape of a Greek cross (equal arms) works well with the altar or Lord's Table placed in the centre. The worship area can be decorated with flowers or greenery, and

candles. The crosses which people have made are displayed on an altar or table, the collages on the walls or on screens. This group should also plan a suitable way of sharing the peace, and the blessing of crosses if desired. But any movement within the liturgy needs to be well orchestrated. The dismissal at the end of the service is important in drawing the whole workshop together and in sending people out to love and serve God.

6 – Greek cross

Session 8

Cross Liturgy as devised by participants takes up the second half of the morning, lasting roughly an hour, with the different groups each playing their part as prepared. Copies of the liturgy must be made available to all so that they know the sequence of their contributions.

Handout 20
Additional Exercises with Crosses

Both crosses and pictures can be used in these exercises; the internet and reference works on religious art are useful resources, as are postcards. The exercises can be done

- as part of an extended time away as on Retreat
- as a one-off experience for any Christian group
- as part of a course on crosses for any faith group.

Exercise no. 1: Questions focusing on faith and mission

- Choose a cross, or a picture of one, which most inspires your personal faith. After silent reflection, share in pairs.
- In a group, choose a cross, or a picture of one, which expresses the mission of your church or Christian fellowship. Share in pairs.
- Compare the different crosses or pictures chosen by your group. Is there a common theme relating to mission? What are the significant differences? Group discussion.
- Collages can be made by the group which reflect their understanding of mission as focused on the cross.

Exercise no. 2: Making a visual mission statement with crosses

- Select one of the crosses or pictures to be used as a visual mission statement for your church or Christian fellowship group.
- In small groups, take turns in explaining your choice and in defending its suitability as symbolizing mission. Passion is a key element in the process with animated debate being encouraged.
- Choose one of the group's crosses or pictures to depict a visual statement of mission for your faith community. (This should be easily understood by non-churchgoers without any explanation.)
- If a group has problems in deciding on one image or cross, they can make a composite representation embracing their different views.

Plenary Session

A spokesperson from each group reports back to the whole gathering, explaining how and why they made their final choice. Time permitting, the different groups can vie with each other in getting their respective picture or cross selected as *the* visual mission statement for their church or Christian fellowship.

Exercise no. 3: Exploring crosses in your church

This exercise is helpful in unlocking the story of a church. It is particularly useful with Sunday school children, a fellowship group like the Mothers' Union, confirmation candidates, seekers, or newcomers, as it can be followed by teaching or discussion on the meaning of the cross in our lives.

Working in pairs, participants are asked to list all the crosses they can find within the building. These could be on stained-glass windows, the altar, altar linen and frontals, statues, font, kneelers, banners, pictures, a rood, reredos, wall paintings, stone and wood work, processional crosses, preaching desk or pulpit. After comparing people's findings, the following questions can be considered:

- How do the crosses reflect the churchmanship of our congregation? Are there crucifixes as well as crosses? Discuss the difference.
- Are the crosses in significant places to reflect the life of the church in prayer, worship, mission and service?
- Are there any interesting stories which relate to the history of the crosses? How old are they? Where do they come from?
- Young people could be asked to draw pictures of their favourite crosses and say what has appealed to them. The facilitator could then provide information about crosses using the drawings as examples.

Crosses in a church provide a readily available focus for prayer and meditation. Prayer cards can be left near some of them to encourage more people to become part of a praying community; the lifeblood of a church. Votive candles close to a cross are an added attraction.

Exercise no. 4: The cross as a flower festival theme

Focusing on the cross in a flower festival would be a novel way of doing theology together, through flowers. Before the event, a short course on crosses together with biblical reflection would give the whole enterprise a solid theological grounding. During the festival, the contributors themselves could explain how their arrangements express the mission of God as seen through the cross. Too often such opportunities for sharing our faith are overlooked. Moreover, this would be a good way of affirming the ministry of flower arrangers, so often the butt of snide remarks.

Exercise no. 5: Things to do with crosses

- Make a cross with a personal intent – for someone who is seriously ill, bereaved, made redundant; a lonely older person; a prisoner; someone struggling with difficult issues; refugees or asylum-seekers; a newcomer to church; baptismal parents; confirmation candidates; a newly ordained or retiring minister.
- Draw a big cross and then stick photos of everyone in your church around it. Place in a quiet area with a list of names so that people can be prayed for individually. Occasional updating is needed.

Exercise no. 6: Bible study

'Though he was in the form of God, [Jesus] did not regard equality with God as something to be exploited, but emptied himself, taking the form of a slave, being born in human likeness. And being found in human form, he humbled himself and became obedient to the point of death – even death on a cross' (Philippians 2.6–8).

The upsetting thing about the gospel to those in authority, both religious and political, at the time of Jesus was the depiction of the Almighty as a humble God. What does that say about the divisions within our denominations; and the power struggles within our own congregations?

38 – Man lying on a broken cross

Notes

1 Hodgson, *The Faith We See.*

2 Collect for Holy Cross Day, *A New Zealand Prayer Book. He Karakia Mihinare o Aotearoa*, 1988, Auckland: Collins for the Anglican Church in Aotearoa, New Zealand and Polynesia, p. 688. (By permission.)

3 John S. Pobee, 1992, 'Stumbling-block, Folly, Good News', in *The Scandal of the Cross: Evangelism and Mission Today,* edited by Wendy Robins and Gillian Hawney, London: USPG: Anglicans in World Mission, p. 79.

4 Collect for Holy Cross Day, *A New Zealand Prayer Book. He Karakia Mihinare o Aotearoa*, p. 688. (By permission.)

5 *Patterns for Worship*, 1995, London: Church House Publishing.

6 *The Alternative Service Book, 1980.* London: SPCK et al. See also 'The Proclamation of the Cross' during a Good Friday service in *Lent, Holy Week, Easter,* 1984, London: Church House Publishing, pp. 207–11.

7 John Bell, *Many and Great. Songs of the World Church*, vol. 1, 1990, and *Sent by the Lord: Songs of the World Church*, vol. 2, 1991, Glasgow: Wild Goose Publications.

7

THE WAY OF THE CROSS

The following programme provides different activities for a half-day event. Otherwise, it can be extended to a full day event by allowing more time for reflection during the two exercises.

Programme for a Half-Day Event

10 minutes:	Welcome and introduction to the programme.
10 minutes:	Opening Worship with Meditation.
10 minutes:	Talk on the Stations of the Cross – Handout 21.
1 hour:	Exercise 1: Doing theology together through art – a group discussion on individual interpretations of a set of Stations.
15 minutes:	Tea break.
1½ hours:	Exercise 2: Biblical references relating to the Stations with reflection being done individually or as a group (this can be continued later as on a Quiet Day or Retreat).
30 minutes:	Eucharist or Denominational Worship.

A large wooden cross can be placed on its side in front of the group with a crown of thorns hanging over the top end and draped with a purple cloth. Appropriate music, such as the 'Stabat Mater' or one of the many Requiems by well-known composers, can be played softly at the start.

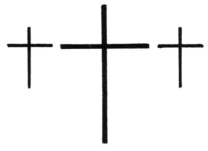

29 – Set of three crosses

Opening Worship with Meditation

'I have been crucified with Christ, and it is no longer I who live, but it is Christ who lives in me;' (Galatians 2.19b–20).

Leader	Come, let us walk with Jesus
All	along the path of sorrow through the City of David.
Leader	Behold, he is walking towards Calvary
All	bent under the weight of the rugged cross.
Leader	He stumbles, falls, rises and stumbles,
All	from Station to Station, bleeding yet blessing.
Leader	Lo, Jesus walks to his death for us
All	as we stand by and jeer at him.
Leader	Shall we help carry the cross?
All	Shall we be like Simon of Cyrene?
Leader	Come, let us walk the walk of Jesus
All	as he walks to his death to bring us life. Amen.

A short time of quiet reflection and prayer.

Meditation
A Special Lenten Fast from South America
Give up harsh words: use generous ones.

Give up unhappiness: take up gratitude.

Give up anger: take up gentleness and patience.

Give up pessimism: take up hope and optimism.

Give up worrying: take up trust in God.

Give up complaining: value what you have.

Give up stress: take up prayer.

Give up judging others: discover Jesus within them.

Give up sorrow and bitterness: fill your heart with joy.

Give up selfishness: take up compassion for others.

Give up being unforgiving: learn reconciliation.

Give up words: fill yourself with silence, and listen to others.[1]

Handout 21
The Stations of the Cross

The Stations or Way of the Cross of Our Lord Jesus Christ were brought to Europe by the Crusaders. While in Jerusalem they had revived a tradition, dating back to the fourth century, in which they followed in the footsteps of Jesus from the judgement seat of Pontius Pilate to Golgotha and the Holy Sepulchre. After the Crusaders left Jerusalem, at the end of the thirteenth century, Franciscan monks remained the guardians of the holy places associated with the *Via Dolorosa* or the Way of Sorrows, and formalized the customary route followed by pilgrims ever since.

Once the Crusaders returned home they wanted to share something of this profound spiritual experience, recognizing that the journey to the Holy Land, whether by land or sea, was too arduous and too dangerous for most people to undertake themselves. Consequently, small sets of Stations were set up across Europe. The first sets were laid out in the open, over rough ground, so that pilgrims walking them would experience some of the humiliation, physical effort and pain suffered by Our Lord as he carried the beam of his cross to Calvary. To heighten the sense of identification, some Ways were built up steep and rocky hills, and the pilgrims would walk with bare feet, crawl on their knees, or carry heavy wooden crosses.

To make them more accessible, paintings, sculptures or carvings depicting the Stations were placed around the walls of churches or else set up at intervals along paths in a churchyard. This has allowed successive generations of Christians to retrace the *Via Dolorosa* in a pilgrimage of penance and prayer. This tradition is followed by Roman Catholics, high-church Anglicans, some Lutherans, and the Eastern Orthodox Church of the Western Rite. The customary celebration of the Stations is on Good Friday, with the Fridays during Lent being added in the Catholic tradition.

The earliest sets grew in number from eight to 36; but in the sixteenth century the Roman Catholic Church finally approved 14 Stations: nine scenes from the gospel and five from folk tradition. The Second Vatican Council added a 15th Station, the resurrection of Jesus from the dead. Other versions may include Jesus' institution of the Eucharist, his praying in the Garden of Gethsemane, appearing before the Sanhedrin, being scourged and crowned with thorns, promising heaven to the repentant thief, and entrusting his mother, Mary, and John to each other.

Bible readings, meditations, hymns and prayers are all part of the liturgical celebration of the Stations, while drama can add much to the overall impact. The liturgy is often accompanied by the singing of the medieval Gregorian chant, *Stabat*

Mater Dolorosa, a meditation on the suffering of Mary during Jesus' crucifixion – 'At the Cross her station keeping stood the mournful Mother weeping, close to Jesus to the last . . .' The poem has been set to music by many composers including Haydn, Palestrina and Rossini.

In recent years a good number of British artists have been inspired to sculpt, carve or paint sets of Stations in churches around the country as a contemporary reflection on the Way of the Cross. The non-verbal depiction of the Stations is seen as a way of doing theology together through art.[2] The exercise 'Doing Theology Through Art' would be particularly appropriate during Lent.

Doing Theology Through Art

This exercise is open to all with no special expertise being required; but Handout 22 provides a useful checklist for the customary set of Stations in any church. A set of pictures could also be used, being passed round the group and then displayed for all to see.

- Members of the group spend some time having a look at each of the Stations in turn.
- They then come together in small groups to discuss their individual interpretations of the Passion as portrayed by the artist.

Handout 22
Biblical References Relating to the Stations of the Cross

These biblical reflections are among those most frequently used. They can be reflected on individually or in a group, preferably before a set of Stations or set of pictures.

---

1. Jesus is condemned to death – Matthew 27.15–26; Mark 14.53–65, 15.1–15; Luke 23.13–25; John 19.4–16
2. Jesus takes up his cross – Matthew 11.29–31; Mark 15.20
3. Jesus falls the first time – Isaiah 42.1–3, 53.6–12
4. Jesus meets his mother – Luke 2.22–35; John 19.25–27

5. Simon of Cyrene helps Jesus carry the cross – Isaiah 52.14; Matthew 27.31–32; Mark 15.21; Luke 23.26
6. Veronica wipes Jesus' face with her veil – Isaiah 53.2–5, 14–15
7. Jesus falls the second time – Hebrews 5.7–10; Isaiah 53.2–3, 8
8. Jesus meets the women of Jerusalem – Luke 23.27–31
9. Jesus falls the third time – Psalm 42.9–11; Romans 7.15–25
10. Jesus is stripped of his garments – Mark 15.24; John 19.23–24
11. Crucifixion: Jesus is nailed to the cross – Mark 15.22–28; Luke 23.33–43; John 19.28–30
12. Jesus dies on the cross – Matthew 27.45–55; Mark 15.33–41; Luke 23.44–49; John 19.28–30
13. Jesus' body is taken down from the cross – Matthew 27.57–58; Mark 15.42–45; Luke 23.50–52; John 19.38–39
14. Jesus is laid in the tomb – Matthew 27.59–66; Mark 15.46–47; Luke 23.53–56; John 19.40–42
15. Jesus rises from the dead – Matthew 28.1–10; Mark 16.1–8; Luke 24.1–12; John 20.1–29

Identify which Stations come from the gospel and which from folk tradition.

39 – 11th Station from Bloemfontein church, South Africa

40 – Fenwick Lawson's Pietà 2

Dramatization of the Passion

Mel Gibson's film, *The Passion of the Christ* (2004), provides an all too graphic depiction of the Way of the Cross, as do some of the Good Friday rituals in the Philippines where men are actually nailed to a cross. Even so, dramatic presentations are popular throughout the world. In contrast to the formal productions at Oberammergau in Austria once every ten years, African villagers will turn out en masse to provide a communal re-enactment of the Passion for their own spiritual edification. A striking example of an African version of the Stations was witnessed by me along the dusty gravel roads of Zimbabwe.

The annual week-long celebration, commemorating Bernard Mizeki at his shrine in Marondera, was led by Bishop Dinis Sengulane, Anglican Bishop of Lebombo in Mozambique. In following the Way, clergy and laity took turns in carrying a large wooden cross while several hundred uniformed Mothers' Union women led the singing, swaying rhythmically as they walked. As we passed alongside fields of corn, women with babies on their backs left their hoeing to accompany us, as did schoolchildren and men on horseback. At each Station, Bishop Dinis gave a short homily linking Jesus' suffering to the everyday experiences of the ever-growing crowd, followed by prayer. The final part of the pilgrimage took us through thorn bushes up a rocky hill, the cross being planted at the top for all to see.

Another time I witnessed a dramatic re-enactment of the Passion in an informal settlement in South Africa. Local youngsters took the leading roles as we followed them through the mud and squalor of passageways between crudely built shacks of cardboard, iron sheets, plastic, and bits of wood. Again, a large crowd of locals were drawn in to relive the story, and to swell the singing of familiar African hymns in spontaneous support, punctuated by the beat of rhythmic movement.

British weather does not encourage outdoor drama yet a good number of church groups brave the elements each year to re-enact the Passion in town centres to great effect. Other tried and tested ideas are a procession of witness on Good Friday that has people following behind a cross through the streets and into a church, or a Passion play that leads people to Stations in various venues such as churches, halls and schools. This can be a powerful experience for those involved and an evangelistic opportunity to engage curious onlookers in discussion.

A good selection of material is available for presenting the Passion narrative in dramatized form, with advice on how best to use the texts with a number of readers.[3] John Bell and Graham Maule from the Iona Community have recorded a collection of songs for Lent and Easter;[4] while USPG: Anglicans in World Mission have put together liturgies and meditations from different countries.[5] New publications on the Stations of the Cross appear regularly, some illustrated or containing liturgical material. The Roman Catholic aid agency, CAFOD, focuses annually on a particular theme such as the violation of human rights, ecology, racism, debt and justice, or on a particular country. These link the cross of Jesus with contemporary situations and provide a window on a wider world.

A Good Friday Service Using Pictures of the Passion

In a Good Friday service, pictures portraying the *Via Dolorosa* can also be used to bring the story alive. The Benedictine Nuns of Turvey Abbey have produced a set of brightly coloured, modern Stations of the Cross. Other sets are found on cards or in illustrated booklets. The images should be spread out beforehand on tables in the aisles around the church to allow easy access. After the reading of one of the

Passion narratives, members of the congregation are invited to choose a picture and meditate on the following questions.

> - Why did I choose this particular picture?
> - What aspect of the Passion spoke to me, or drew me to the picture itself?

It could be that one is denying Christ like Peter; carrying the cross with Simon of Cyrene; watching with the weeping women of Jerusalem; grieving with the women at the foot of the cross; repenting with the good thief; or even being with Jesus himself on the cross. Before continuing with the service, sharing may take place between people sitting next to each other, but one must respect those who prefer to keep silent and continue with their meditation.

Making Your Own Stations of the Cross

In 2009 the artist Mark Cazalet was invited to involve members of the many different groups who come through St Andrew's church, Fulham Fields in London, in making their own set of Stations in a concentrated two week period prior to Lent. These included the homeless, the Mums and Toddlers group, a fruit-and-vegetable co-operative, coffee morning people, and members of the congregation. It was hoped that the joint effort would foster mutual identification between the groups, as well as exploring the creative potential of both individuals and the community as a whole. Setting the Gospels in the context of people's everyday lives, Cazalet wished to affirm the relevance of Christ's suffering and resurrection in their midst, and to create a communal reflection on Christ's Passion.

Preparations included precise planning, meeting the different groups to assess their capabilities, and the collecting together of all the necessary materials including the recycling of Christmas festival debris. The Stations were mounted on birch ply boards on a shaped cradle, ten of which were strapped over foam to nave pillars, while the other five were sited in the chancel and Lady Chapel.[6]

During the workshops, one of the more reluctant 'homeless' became totally absorbed in making a cross by fixing a soup spoon and two teaspoons onto a wooden base to represent Christ's head and hands. The mothers identified with St Veronica by making rubbings of Christ's head situated in the church, which were then printed on tea towels and hung on a washing line. While the Sunday school children got the feeling of Christ's hands being pierced by hammering nails into cut-outs of their own hands, which had been imprinted on kitchen sponges.

Cazalet believes that the project was a truly memorable experience for all those involved.[7]

Handout 23
Suggestions for making your own Stations

Guidelines for facilitators: These activities are designed for different groups of all ages to complete over a number of weeks. When completed, the visual displays would need to be placed in correct order either on a wall, pillars or stands, with the other Stations being set up in between. Each of the Stations should have the right number placed alongside it, together with its title.

1. Jesus is condemned to death

Resources: Large candle, metal base, length of barbed wire.
Activity: The candle is set firmly on the base with the wire wound spirally round it and lit during services.

41 – Amnesty Candle, Salisbury Cathedral

2. Jesus takes up his cross

Resources: Different colours of powder paint, flour, water, paint or baking trays, sheet of newsprint or newspapers.
Boil about 2lbs flour in water to make a thick consistency. Add different colours of paint to the mixture in separate containers. Paint can also be mixed with wallpaper paste. Work on a board or strong card.
Activity: Children place their feet in a tray of paint and then walk along a pathway on the newsprint or newspaper to represent Jesus' starting along the road to Calvary.

3. Jesus falls the first time

Resources: From Station 2.
Activity: A large finger painting is made of Jesus falling under a heavy cross. He is surrounded by smaller finger paintings of each one of us staggering under our little crosses.

4. Jesus meets his mother

Resources: Newsprint or A5 paper; felt tip pens, paint or crayons.
Activity: Children's drawings of their mothers are placed around a large central cross.

5. Simon of Cyrene helps Jesus carry the cross

Resources and Activity: Make your own little cross from sticks, wood, wire, pipe cleaners, tongue depressors (these can be decorated), etc. Some are placed alongside a large cross lying on its side, made of bare tree branches or two pieces of wood tied together. Others are used in Station 12.

6. Veronica wipes Jesus' face with her veil

Resources: Large sheet of paper, picture of Jesus' face, small pieces of coloured sticky paper or real mosaics, felt tip pens.
Activity: Make a Mandala by placing the picture of Jesus' face in the centre of the page and then designing a pattern around it with felt tip pens. This is filled in with small pieces of coloured sticky paper or mosaics. For information on Mandalas: http://en.wikipedia.org/wiki/Mandala.

7. Jesus falls the second time

Resources: Cardboard; glue; a collection of 'fallen' material – string bags, bottle tops, rubbish, papers, small plastic containers, sweet papers, etc.
Activity: Glue the fallen objects onto a strong cardboard base. Overlap shapes as texture is important. Can be done in the shape of a cross.

8. Jesus meets the women of Jerusalem

Resources: Newspapers, magazines, church publications; newsprint or A5 sheet of paper; scissors; glue sticks.
Activity: Cut out pictures of women weeping or in situations of suffering. Make a collage by pasting pictures onto a large piece of paper, with these verses in the centre: '*A great number of the people followed him, and among them were women who were beating their breasts and wailing for him. But Jesus turned to them and said, "Daughters of Jerusalem, do not weep for me, but weep for yourselves and for your children."*' (Luke 23.27–28)

9. Jesus falls the third time

Resources: Thick cardboard; sieved sand; powder paints; glue.
Activity: Draw a picture using symbols for Christ (fish, anchor, ship's mast, different crosses, candle, vine, etc.). Add different powder paints to the sand and sprinkle on glued sections of the drawings. Pour off excess sand.

10. Jesus is stripped of his garments

Resources: Self-hardening clay – Mix together 1½ cups salt and 4 cups flour in a bowl. Add 1½ cups water gradually to form a ball. Knead until it sticks together. (Plasticine is a more expensive alternative.)
Activity: Make simple figures out of the clay. Allow to dry for about two days. Group together on a board with a small pile of rags nearby.

11. Crucifixion: Jesus is nailed to the cross

Resources: Kitchen sponges, felt tip pens, powder paint mix (as above), nails, a few hammers, sharp knife.
Activity: Follow Cazalet's idea of getting children to place their hands on kitchen sponges and draw round them with felt tip pens. These are coloured in as desired. Alternatively, make hand prints on the sponges using the powder paint mixture

above. Cut the shapes out and then hammer nails into them to get the feeling of Christ's hands being pierced with nails.

12. Jesus dies on the cross

Resources: A hanger and fishing line; different coloured pieces of felt; needles and thread; scissors.
Activity: Different sizes of fish are made from the felt, and then hung from the hanger with fishing line to make a carefully balanced mobile. (The Greek word for fish, *ichthus*, was an ancient Christian symbol, the Greek characters standing for 'Jesus Christ, Son of God, Saviour'.)

13. Jesus' body is taken down from the cross

Resources: Hessian or blanket, boxes; nightlights.
Activity: A hill is made by covering stacked boxes with hessian or a blanket. A pathway is made up the side of the mound to show The Way to Calvary. Nightlights are placed at intervals to mark the Stations. A large cross or crucifix is placed at the top. Some of the little crosses from Station 5 can be fixed in a sand tray to make a hill of crosses. (If used in the reading of the Gospel story, as on Good Friday, then the nightlights can be lit one by one to mark The Way.)

14. Jesus is laid in the tomb

Resources: Pieces of slate or 4 flat stones and a round stone; fresh flowers and greenery for making a small garden. *Papier mâché* can also be used.
Activity: Make a cave from the flat stones or *papier mâché* with a round stone covering the entrance. Stand on a large tray surrounded by sand, flowers and greenery, and place at the foot of the hill. A play dough figure can be bound in a bandage inside the tomb.

15. Jesus rises from the dead

Resources: For 2 puppets – 2 polystyrene balls on sticks for the heads (or 2 ping pong balls, or stocking or sock stuffed with cotton wool); 2 crosspiece (kebab) sticks for shoulders; some suitable clothing.
Activity: The puppets are made by fixing the head onto a stick, with another stick placed across it for shoulders. One represents Jesus and the other, Mary Magdalene. Simple clothing is hung from the shoulders of the 2 figures. Faces can

be painted onto the headpieces, and wool glued on for hair. The figures are placed in the garden outside the cave. The entrance stone can be set to one side.

12 – Traditional crucifix

Handout 24
Additional Exercises

Exercise no. 1: Discussion using films on the Passion

A good number of films focus on the Passion. Either the whole film or clips can be used to initiate discussion.

King of Kings. Nicholas Ray, 1961;
The Gospel According to St Matthew. Pier Paolo Pasolini, 1964;
The Greatest Story Ever Told. George Stevens, 1965;
Jesus Christ Superstar (rock opera). Norman Jewison, 1973;
Life of Brian (comedy). Terry Jones, 1979;
The Last Temptation of Christ. Martin Scorsese, 1988;
Jesus of Montreal. Denys Arcand, 1989;
The Passion of the Christ. Mel Gibson, 2004.

- How faithfully do you think the Passion was portrayed in the films you viewed? Discuss any criticisms or new insights.
- What do you feel about the presentation of the Passion in a modern context, or as a rock opera or comedy? How does this affect your response?

Exercise no. 2: Discussion of Handel's interpretation of the Crucifixion

Listen to the solo and chorus 'He was despised and rejected of men', and 'Surely He hath borne our griefs and sorrows' from Handel's *Messiah*.

Alto Solo: He was despised and rejected of men; a man of sorrows, and acquainted with grief . . . He hid not his face from shame and spitting. (Isaiah 53.3)

Chorus: Surely He hath borne our griefs, and carried our sorrows! He was wounded for our transgressions; He was bruised for our iniquities; the chastisement of our peace was upon Him. And with His stripes we are healed. (Isaiah 53.4–5)

- Discuss how the composer has interpreted the Crucifixion through words and music.
- Why do you think *Messiah* has such a continued appeal to believers and non-believers alike?

Notes

1 Anonymous, 'A Special Lenten Fast' in *CAFOD Prayer Pack, Easter 2009*. (By permission.)

2 Barbara Taylor, 2000, 'Stations of the Cross' in *Stations: The new sacred art*, Bury St Edmunds Art Gallery, p. 11. See also Bishop Crispin Hollis, 2000, *Stations of the Cross: Reflections on Portsmouth Stations*.

3 E.g. *Common Worship: Proclaiming the Passion*, 2007, London: Church House Publishing; *Lent, Holy Week, Easter*, pp. 117–75.

4 John Bell and Graham Maule, 1996, *The Courage to Say No*, with CD. Glasgow: Wild Goose Publications, pp. 30–43.

5 E.g. 'We Wait: Litany for Good Friday' in *Let All the World*, pp. 31–2; 'Good Friday' from 'Chinese Meditations for Christmas and Easter' in *From Shore to Shore*, pp. 49–50.

6 See Cazalet's report with photos by Kate Keara Pelen: http://www.standrewsfulham. com/art/stations2009/stations2009.html

7 Report by Katy Hounsell-Roberts, *Church Times*, 13/3/2009.

PART 4

PRAYING AT THE FOOT OF THE CROSS

On Retreat or Quiet Day the talks can be spread over a longer period with more time being given for silent reflection.

Programme for Full Day (timing is flexible)

10 minutes:	Welcome and introduction to programme.
5 minutes:	Opening Worship.
30 minutes:	Talk on 'Making the Sign of the Cross' – Handout 25.
30 minutes:	Reflection and/or Discussion.
15 minutes:	Tea break.
10 minutes:	Short Worship followed by silence.
15 minutes:	Talk on 'Prayer as Holy Silence' – Handout 26.
30 minutes:	Bible Study with time for reflection.
10 minutes:	Talk on 'Prayer as Presence' – Handout 27.
30 minutes:	Topics for Discussion (if desired).
	Eucharist or Denominational Worship.
	Lunch break and rest period in silence.
1½ hours:	Short Worship – Talk on Meditation – Handout 28.
	Meditation practice.
15 minutes:	Tea break.
30 minutes:	Praying with a Holding Cross – Handout 29.
30 minutes:	Talk on Labyrinths, Prayer Stations, Street Retreats – Handout 30.
	Closure with Evening Prayers or Compline.

8

MAKING THE SIGN OF THE CROSS

Opening Worship

> *'Let them praise his name with dancing' (Psalm 149.3).*
>
> **Leader** Let us pray with our mind and hearts,
> **All**   and with our souls.
> **Leader** Come, let us pray with our bodies,
> **All**   for they are temples of our spirits.
> **Leader** Dance, you children of the resurrection.
> **All**   Leap like David before the Holy Ark.
> **Leader** Sitting, standing, lying and walking,
> **All**   may our ceaseless prayers rise to the living God,
>   Father, Son and Holy Spirit. Amen.
>
> Followed by a short time of silence

Handout 25
Talk on Making the Sign of the Cross

Little Sign and Big Sign

The biblical origin of making the sign of the cross (hereafter referred to as the Sign) is found in Deuteronomy 6.48 where pious Hebrews are enjoined to wear the scriptural injunction 'to love God with heart, mind and soul' on their arms and between their eyes. From this comes the orthodox Jewish custom of tying sacred

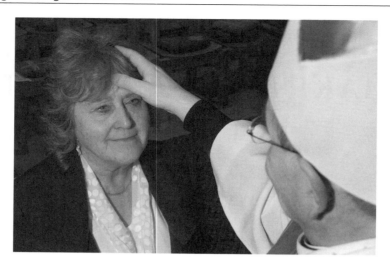

42 – Bishop's Confirmation

phylacteries on the forehead and arms. The signing on the forehead as the mark of their special relationship to God is also mentioned in Revelation 7.3, 9.4 and 14.1.

The first recorded reference to the Sign in a Christian context is attributed to the church father Tertullian (AD 160–225). He observed that 'We Christians wear out our foreheads with the sign of the cross.' The ritual accompanied all the normal acts of daily life such as coming in and going out, putting on shoes, eating, bathing, lighting candles, lying down, sitting up, and so on.

The first evidence of the Sign being extended to other parts of the body dates from fourth-century Georgia, Russia. Legend has it that St Nino healed a reigning queen by prayerfully touching her head, shoulders and feet with her wooden cross. The first known association of the Sign with Jesus himself is depicted in a sixth-century Ravenna mosaic where he is portrayed as making it in the stylized manner of a priest.

Crossing oneself, blessing oneself, signing oneself – all these mean the same thing as making a sign of the cross. At first, believers made the Sign on their foreheads with the bare thumb. This gesture is sometimes called the Little Sign, and is still practised in various rites as in marking with an ash cross on Ash Wednesday, in anointing with holy oil in the sacrament of Confirmation, and in blessing the grievously ill and the dying with holy unction. A variation of the Little Sign is observed with the upward thumb laid across the horizontal forefinger, and devoutly pressed against the lips, thus forming an image of the cross.

There are numerous options for the positioning of the fingers of the right hand in the so-called Big Sign, as for example:

- The first three fingers held upright (symbolizing the Trinity) with the other two bent and pressed against the palm (symbolic of the descent of Christ from heaven to earth and also his twin natures, divine and human);
- A threefold movement in which the three joined fingers touch the forehead to sanctify the mind, the navel to sanctify feelings, and both shoulders to sanctify the body. The hand is then dropped alongside the body followed by a short bow. The Signing is synchronized with the invocation of the Trinitarian formula: 'in the name of the Father, the Son and the Holy Spirit';
- A common variation has all five fingers held together and upright signifying the five wounds of Christ.

5 – Latin cross

The Saving Power of the Sign

Over the centuries the Sign has continued to fulfil several functions in the individual and collective lives of believers. It serves

- as both a mini-creed and a missionary proclamation in invoking the Trinity and confessing the Christian faith.
- as a formula for a verbal exorcism to drive out evil spirits from oneself, other people, afflicted animals and haunted places.
- as a mantra for prayer and meditation, being repeated either silently or aloud so as to focus the mind on our spiritual union with the crucified and risen Christ.
- as a Christian form of blessing reserved for priests.
- as a reminder of our baptism, and the protection we enjoy, when used together with holy water from the stoup or font in a church.
- as a visible mode of administering healing to those sick in body, mind and spirit.
- as a rite to sanctify and consecrate persons, animals, objects and sites in the name of the Triune God.
- as a way of petitioning for divine favours, e.g. footballers making the Sign before a game, potters blessing clay before working with it, housewives blessing food as it goes into the oven.
- as an act of revolutionary defiance as happened when Christian worship was banned under Communist rule in Romania. Believers made the Sign by silently moving the tongue inside the mouth.
- as the definitive gesture in bidding farewell to a departed person.
- as a convenient liturgical device to commence and conclude prayers as well as services.
- as a prayer for protection against adversaries, as with St Benedict, 'By the sign of the cross, deliver me from my enemies, O Lord.'

For Celtic Christians, the cross of Christ was their one true weapon against evil, seen and unseen, which was thought to surround them.[1] They made the Sign as a way of commending themselves and their chores to God, and in praying for his protection throughout their daily lives. Oral tradition is rich in blessings and invocations using the Sign whether this be in milking a cow, baking bread, or petitioning God for healing. Similarly, Bor Dinka Christians in Sudan believe that 'marking with the sign of the cross' in baptism will protect them against evil and misfortune, particularly that sent by vindictive ancestral divinities whom they have renounced.

In the wake of the Reformation, the Sign was rejected by many Protestant Churches as a vestige of Roman Catholicism, but Catholics and Anglicans continued to use it. The *Book of Common Prayer* included it in the baptism service, and the Anglican Canon Law of 1604 acknowledged it. In his Small Catechism, Martin Luther insisted on its usage at morning and evening prayer, and in his Order of Baptism of 1526. He even said, 'When you get out of bed, bless yourself with the holy cross in the name of the Trinity.' In the United Methodist Church, the Sign is becoming more widely accepted, the Elders touching the laity on their foreheads. As an ecumenical symbol, the Sign could help us recover our sense of collective baptismal union with Christ, in his death and resurrection.

For the Anglo-Catholic clergy of the Society of the Holy Cross in Britain, their daily prayer begins with the words 'We should glory in the Cross of our Lord Jesus Christ.' Further on, the words 'through the saving power of the Cross' are followed with a small +, indicating the point at which those reciting the prayer make the sign of the cross. For the Revd Luke Miller SCC, this gesture 'is a sign of the truth of the Christian life that what is impressed inwardly is what is seen outwardly', through the saving power of the cross. For him, the cross is 'the expression of the depth of God's love', a joyful thing, which infuses their work as mission priests with love and truth as they call others to be saved and made free.[2]

Reflection and/or Discussion

- What part has making the sign of the cross played in your spiritual life? What has it meant to you?
- While making the Sign, how mindful are you of the need to coordinate body, mind, soul and speech?
- Reflect on what St Paul said about the body being the temple of the Holy Spirit within you. (1 Corinthians 6.19)

Notes

1 De Waal, *Every Earthly Blessing*, pp. 126–8.

2 Luke Miller SCC, Vicar of St Mary's, Tottenham, London, writing in *Church Times*, 12/6/2009.

9

PRAYER AND MEDITATION

Worship and Reflection

'The Spirit helps us in our weakness; for we do not know how to pray as we ought, but that very Spirit intercedes with sighs too deep for words.' (Romans 26)

Leader	Amen to the Spirit of the Lord,
All	who prays within our hearts.
Leader	We pray to the Father,
All	not we but Christ within us who prays to him.
Leader	Let us pray in union with all creation,
All	and with the saints of the Lord.
Leader	Let us pray for *shalom* and healing,
All	and for the Kingdom, come Lord Jesus. Amen.

Followed by a time of silence

31 – Peace cross

43 – Khotso House tapestry, Johannesburg

44 – The Power and the Glory by Coral Bernadine

45 – 'You have surrounded me with joy'

Handout 26
Prayer as Holy Silence

Prayer is not something that we do of our own volition. It is the Holy Spirit that prays in and through us (Romans 8.26). This Spirit is from God the Father and from the crucified Lord Jesus Christ. The more we walk with Christ, the more clearly we shall echo the Spirit's sighs together with the groaning of creation (cf. Romans 8.22). In union with Jesus hanging on the cross, our prayer becomes a redemptive cry for healing, sanctification and reconciliation with our heavenly Father (cf. Matthew 27.46). Thus, Christian prayer, unlike any other, is an engagement with the cross of history. In and through our prayer, it becomes the cross of faith here and now in our individual and collective witness.

A classic description of Christian prayer is given by St Paul: 'I have been crucified with Christ; and it is no longer I who live, but it is Christ who lives in me' (Galatians 2.20). Through our faith, Christ comes to dwell in our hearts (cf. Ephesians 3.17). In Christian meditation, unlike the Eastern and New Age varieties, one seeks not to cultivate and refine the ego as an excuse for exploring our human potential for holiness. Instead, one stills the ego and replaces it with what St Paul calls 'the mind of Jesus' (Philippians 2.5). St John the Baptist sums up this mystical relationship with Christ, saying, 'He shall increase and I shall decrease' (John 3.30). In prayer, our ego is gradually taken over by the indwelling Christ himself and, with the Spirit praying through us, we become channels of God's activity. This is reflected in Jesus' own words as he prayed to his heavenly Father in the garden of Gethsemane, 'Not my will but thy will be done' (Luke 22.42).

The umbrella term we use to define Christian prayer is silence. Prayer is the sacrament of stilling the mind. Discursive prayer is associated with words, whether spoken out loud or in silence, as distinct from what Thomas Merton, the Trappist monk, called contemplative prayer. The latter is a prayer of the heart. Naturally, we begin our inner journey with discursive prayer but we should aspire to grow into contemplative stillness.

In our contact with Eastern spirituality, and a subsequent rediscovery of Christian contemplation as practised by our medieval church fathers, silence as a form of prayer is gaining recognition as being central to our private and communal devotions. The Quakers have always anchored their worship in silence, occasionally punctuated with inspired utterances. Silence, however, is not a mere absence of words. It lacks authenticity if our mind continues to chatter like a monkey. True prayerful silence crucifies the ego. Each time we observe silence, whether in our private devotions or liturgical worship, we need reminding to internalize the spirit of the cross.

Another distinctive mark of Christian silence is that it transcends human labels. Speaking to the Phoenician woman, Jesus observes that while her people prayed on the holy mountain and Jews in the holy city of Jerusalem, true prayer is said in the Spirit alone (cf. John 4.20–24). Too often, we have tended to make God in our own image, answerable to a list of petitions. Of course, we shall never see God as he truly is but we aspire to see as much of his transcendent nature as possible. In silence, we jettison our prejudices based on gender, race, and culture, and visualize God as the One who died for us all. This is the radical nature of true Christian prayer.

Bible Study No. 3

'At daybreak he [Jesus] departed and went into a deserted place. And the crowds were looking for him; and when they reached him, they wanted to prevent him from leaving them' (Luke 4.42).

Jesus knew well how to strike the balance between his engagement with the demands of the world and his prayer life. How balanced is your Christian life? How do you cope with some of the challenges?

Handout 27
Prayer as Presence

It was St John of the Cross (1542–91), the Spanish mystic, who sought to approach God using the mode called *via negativa*, the negative way. Accordingly, in our prayer and meditation we remove layer after layer of our misconceptions about the nature of God, and pray to him as the God of pure love and impartial justice. God the Father of the crucified Jesus is, in the words of St John of the Cross, 'neither this nor that'. He is beyond all our opinions and preferences. For St John, a prayer on the cross leads us into a 'bright darkness'. This is not the darkness of inertia and ignorance, but the darkness of total surrender to the will of God. Here, we submit ourselves to God alone and not to the tempting propositions of the world. Prayer is, thus, less about us talking to God and more about waiting on him in silence, and listening to his still small voice.

Our intellect stands in the way of us getting close to God and God getting close to work within us. Praying in darkness, born of faith and surrender, compels us to empty ourselves of all imaginary idols and slowly to enter into our heart. By heart we do not mean subjective emotions. The heart in Christian prayer stands for love, compassion, joy, innocence, humility, contrition, tenderness, and a burning zeal for the Kingdom. Mystics of the Orthodox tradition exhort us to let the mind move away from the head and descend into the heart, beyond words and techniques.

Prayer informed by the spirit of the cross emphasizes the Being rather than the Doing or Thinking aspect of the human personality. In the West, our Christian life is so often oriented towards busyness rather than a simple beingness. Whether it is worship, mission, good works, interfaith dialogue or even prayer, it is something that we feel we are called to do: an action or an enterprise, with prayer just added to the list.

Prayer of the cross is not something that we do from time to time like taking a prescription pill. True Christian prayer is presence. This has nothing to do with physical presence or charisma. Rather, it is an inner presence: a constant, ongoing outpouring of love directed at God; and, in response to God's love, it touches and transforms everything that we do, say, think and feel. This presence is what St Paul calls 'ceaseless prayer' (1 Thessalonians 4.17), and is the goal of Christian spirituality. Prayer, then, becomes effortless and second nature: something that we are in body, mind and spirit. In the words of St Paul, let us ask God for the blessing that we may grow to 'pray in the Spirit at all times in every prayer and supplication' (Ephesians 6.18).

Topics for Discussion

- Share your best experience of feeling close to God – in a church, during meditation, on a walk, by the sea, listening to music, reading a book, in fellowship with someone special, watching living things?
- What gets in the way of feeling close to God? How could this be resolved?
- How do different styles of prayer either help or hinder your spirituality?
- Should silence play a greater role in church worship?

Handout 28
Worship and Talk on Meditation

There is nothing that we humans can initiate to induce true prayer except by opening ourselves up to the crucified and risen Lord Jesus and allowing the Holy Spirit to pray through us. We now offer a few suggestions, not techniques, about approaching the Holy Spirit in meditation. Every Christian is able to engage in such prayer, as all it requires is the use of the heart, not head.

In looking to see how Jesus himself meditated, the Gospels tell us that he would regularly withdraw from people for long periods of time. Matthew 6.5–14 gives us some idea of his method. For Jesus, meditation is a personal, even a private affair, between God and man. His instructions are simple: 'Whenever you pray, go into your room and shut the door and pray to your Father who is in secret.' This prayer is addressed to the crucified God who looks into our hearts and not into our words and gestures.

Jesus then springs a surprise. Instead of mapping out an interior journey, he reveals the Kingdom prayer. From our silence and solitude, we are suddenly propelled into the Kingdom, where daily bread is shared along with forgiveness, and we brace ourselves to face new challenges. In this prayer there is a perfect balance between the heart and responsible action. In meditation, the reality of the cross enables us to discern what we need to do to heal the wounded world. But just going out and engaging in random action, no matter how well-intentioned, would be counterproductive. Action must flow from prayer and prayer must lead to sacrificial living (cf. James 5.16b).

'Whenever you pray, go into your room and shut the door and pray to your Father who is in secret.' (Matthew 6.6)

Leader	Our bodies are temples of our souls.
All	Let us sit still and full of repose.
Leader	Come, let us invoke the Holy Spirit,
All	the author of life, love and peace.
Leader	Hear you, Christ is knocking on the door,
All	let us invite him into the silence of our being.
Leader	We meditate on the beauty of Christ,
All	who dwells within our hearts and minds.
Leader	With every breath we plead with Jesus.
All	We die with him and rise with him.
Leader	May the Lord bless us and keep us,
All	As we pray under the cross of Jesus. Amen.

Suggestions for Meditating

Certain methods may be followed to bring body, mind and soul into focus before beginning to pray with the cross.

- First, practise sitting quietly in a comfortable position for a fixed period of time each day, preferably in the same place and at the same time. Two short spells, morning and evening, suffice. This helps settle the mind into a gentle routine.
- During meditation, one may play music or even chant or sing softly.
- The repetition of Christian *mantras* such as Jesus, Christ, Mary or *shalom* is helpful in stilling the mind; as are scriptural phrases like Hallelujah, *maranatha*, 'I am that I am'; or invocations like 'Come, Lord Jesus,' 'Thy will be done', 'Thy Kingdom come'. The Jesus prayer is strongly recommended – 'Jesus Christ, Son of God, Son of Mary, have mercy on me, a sinner', or its shortened version, 'Lord Jesus, have mercy'.
- For meditation, the chosen cross or crucifix should be large enough to be seen in detail. Sitting quietly, with hands folded or resting in our laps, and with our eyes either open or half closed, we view the cross intently for a while and reflect on what it means to us in terms of our relationship with Christ.
- We then close our eyes and try to visualize the cross within us, internalizing it as a spiritual reality. But we need to remember that the cross is neither an icon nor

an idol, but an instrument to induce an experience of closeness to the crucified Lord deep within our heart.

- In our prayers, we mentally hold onto a specific event, situation, or certain people where we know that there is suffering. In this way, we connect the historic cross of Jesus with the woundedness and alienation in the world around us. Entering into this experience, we ask ourselves to what extent we might be directly or indirectly responsible for the pain that we so clearly see.

- A major component of prayer and meditation on the cross is the nurturing of contrition and the quest for forgiveness. In our mind's eye we remember all those people whom we have hurt or offended at any time. We reflect on the situations where we have failed to trust in God's love for us, and where we have betrayed this trust by not loving God and neighbour enough. We also reflect on the ways in which we have contributed to the ravaging of God's creation and the creatures who inhabit it. We remind ourselves that the risen Christ continues to suffer where there is a breach of peace and harmony.

- After having focused on the pain, we now bring a sense of healing and reconciliation into the situation. Concentrating on this feeling, we try and send it out to those in need together with a sense of penitence and forgiveness. In our prayers,
  - we may invoke the Holy Spirit to enter into a situation and to bless individuals with comfort, peace and protection.
  - we may invite Christ to come and dwell in our hearts and lead us into a sense of at-one-ment with his experience on the cross.
  - we keep returning to the cross, mindful of the connection between the suffering of Christ and the present suffering in the world.

- The next stage is to bring the breath into the process, remembering that the word 'spirit' means breath. Watching the breath is the secret of all meditation; and it will become ever more still as our mind becomes still. By focusing on the outgoing and the incoming breath, its falling and its rising, we die with Christ and we rise with Christ. Although it can be done at any time and anywhere, it is important to use it first in our seated meditation as it will serve to deepen our overall experience of being one with Christ on the cross.

By the end of a session we need to have achieved a sense of forgiveness, freedom and peace of the spirit; become more sensitive to the alienation in the world around us; and gathered enough insight and wisdom to bring a degree of healing by right action to serve the Kingdom. These few suggestions provide a backdrop for meditating on the cross, but the variations are endless and it is up to each person to find a way which suits their spiritual make-up. The most important thing is to practise regularly and consistently. Dry and fruitless periods can be expected, with feelings of boredom and frustration, but perseverance is essential.

Reflection

- Watch your breath while you pray, meditate or read the Scripture. Focus on the breathing prayer as much as possible during the course of the day.
- What part have Quiet Days, Retreats and pilgrimages played in deepening your faith?

Handout 29
Praying with a Holding Cross

A wooden holding cross is also a useful tool in meditation. Made from different woods, the arms of the cross are uneven so as to fit comfortably between the fingers when cradled in the palm of the hand. Commonly used as an aid to prayer, wooden crosses are particularly helpful in providing pastoral care and bringing relief to the dying, the terminally ill and those in distress, when words no longer have much meaning. In encouraging their usage, Angela Ashwin has provided a leaflet with suitable prayers for various occasions. She explains that,

46 – A holding cross

Sometimes, it is enough to hold the cross silently; this is itself prayer. Maybe you have no words anyway, and it is through your sense of touch that you are expressing your love of Christ and your need of him. Holding a cross can also be a way of praying for others, especially those who are suffering. Or it can be helpful to hold a cross when making an act of penitence.[1]

One of Angela's own prayers with a holding cross is as follows:

Jesus, what have you not suffered;
what have you not given for me?
I can never comprehend you,

47 – Holding crosses

and wonder
at the depths of the darkness
which you entered,
and the cost of the love
which you would not betray.[2]

A pocket cross is another aid to prayer carried by millions of people worldwide. The small stitched cross on plastic canvas tucked snugly into its case is often given to mark a friendship or special occasion together with the poem by Verna Mae Thomas beginning with words, 'I carry a cross in my pocket, a simple reminder to me of the fact that I am a Christian, no matter where I may be . . .' When given at a time of bereavement, a white case may be edged in black or purple and accompanied by Henry Scott Holland's poem 'Death is nothing at all'.

Carried in pockets or held in hands, crosses can be a source of great solace and comfort in our society where there is so much loneliness and people have so little time for one another. Under these circumstances, the cross could be our loyal companion, providing us much needed fellowship and affirmation of our faith.

Things To Do

- Pray the news as a group or on your own. Candles or votive lights may be lit as a special intention for named individuals and places.
- Go on a retreat on your own, or organized with a spiritual director. Listen to God and reassess your life.[3]
- Write a letter to God in which you open up your heart and say what you really feel. This could be shared with a friend or with your minister as a confession.

Notes

1 Prayers on *The Holding Cross* are reproduced by kind permission of Angela Ashwin. Handcrosses are available through the internet.

2 Ashwin, *The Holding Cross* leaflet.

3 For more information on retreats: UK National Retreat Association annual publications; info@retreat.org.uk; Christian hospitality across Europe at http://www.christian-hotel.com.

10

LABYRINTHS, PRAYER STATIONS AND A RETREAT ON THE STREETS

Handout 30
Walking a Labyrinth

Walking a labyrinth is an ancient meditative tool found in many different cultures and civilizations from early Crete to India, Egypt to Peru. For as long as 4,000 years, labyrinths have been used as medicine wheels among Native American people, as a symbol of Mother Earth for the Hopi, the 'Never-Ending Circle' of the Celts, a principle of Chinese *feng shui*, a mystical form in *kabalah*, and as floor mosaics by the Romans; but they also have a historic tradition as a symbol of the Christian journey.

Found in medieval cathedrals, and marked out on the floor in coloured stone or tiles, the winding circular route is said to represent the path of the soul through life. During Holy Week in Chartres Cathedral in northern France, early pilgrims followed the famous labyrinth on their knees in a stylized imitation of Jesus' walk to Calvary.[1] It was also ritually acted out on various occasions such as on the eve of a baptism or confirmation, to mark the end of a pilgrimage, or, more usually, as a form of contemplative prayer.

The three main stages in following a labyrinth are the walk in, where one clears and quietens the mind; spending time in the centre in the presence of God; and the walk out, where the experience of encounter with God is taken back into the world. In recent times churches and cathedrals worldwide have revived the use of labyrinths, both inside and outside their buildings, as an aid to contemplative prayer. The internet offers a wealth of advice on different designs, both ancient and modern.[2]

Prayer Stations

The modern idea of a prayer journey has much the same purpose except that a number of imaginative prayer stations are set up in a suitable venue requiring active involvement. This could include lighting a candle, intoning a prayer, composing a prayer and adding it to a prayer tree, reading a poem or biblical text, holding a cross, meditating, responding to imagery, working with paints or clay, listening to music, making something simple like a cross with twigs, and so forth. Written guidance is given as to how the worshipper can interact with the activity at each station.

The stations are placed at intervals, inside a building or in the open. If a particular theme is being followed, as with the Passion, then they need to be visited in sequence, one after another. But in what is called a prayer fayre, they can be visited in any order allowing for easier access and larger numbers. This would be a better option during an act of worship and could become the worship experience itself.[3]

A Retreat on the Streets

A Retreat on the Streets is another form of active meditation. It can be done in several ways but usually starts with worship in a church. Participants are then sent out alone and in silence, with clear instructions as to how to spend their time, and with a map if necessary. They are asked to stop, look, listen and pray at different places:

- where people are present, e.g. crossroads, streets, bus stops, parks, school playgrounds, railway stations;
- where people are being served, e.g. shops, eating places, amusement arcades, pubs;
- where there are signs of destruction, e.g. graffiti, vandalism, litter, car exhaust;
- where there are signs of life, e.g. a tree, a plant pushing up through the paving, flower beds, birds in the sky.

At each point they can respond to what they see and hear by asking themselves,

- Where is God in the busyness of this city, town or village life?
- Where can I see Christ being crucified?
- Where can I see love and compassion?
- How are onlookers responding to my prayerful presence?

The Retreat on the Streets can last a couple of hours or a whole day, with participants being given no more than 50p to spend as a way of identifying with those less fortunate than themselves. The Retreat ends at a specified time with a careful debriefing. This gives people a chance to share their experiences and feelings, and to be given emotional support if needed. Ideally the Retreat should be rounded off liturgically with an *agape*, Eucharist, Evensong, Compline, or informal prayers: mission and worship being brought together at the foot of the cross.

Our prayer is that we may live the cross in every moment of our lives through words, deeds and contemplative presence.

Closing Prayer
Resurrection Hope

May the power of the cross,
the joy of the resurrection,
and the presence of the risen Lord
be with me, and all whom I love, Amen.
(England)[4]

Notes

1 Mimi Spencer. 'Merry go Round' in *Spectator*, 29/9/2007, p. 68. To 'walk' an online labyrinth: www.yfc.co.uk/labyrinth. Pocket-sized finger labyrinths replicating patterns in famous cathedrals are also being used as stress-busting techniques.

2 See 'Further Resources'.

3 For example: Ian Tarrant and Sally Dakin, 2004, *Labyrinths and Prayer Stations*, Grove Books Worship Series 180, Cambridge: Grove Books Ltd; Jonny Baker, Report in *Church Times*, 20/4/2007, and http://jonnybaker.blogs.com; and www.labyrinth.org.uk; www.freshworship.org (alternative worship community at Grace, Ealing, London).

4 Ashwin, *The Holding Cross* leaflet.

FURTHER RESOURCES

Further Reading, Prayers, Meditations

John Ansell, Jenny Hunt, Gerry McFlynn, Gordon Matthews (compilers), 1988, *Prayers for Peacemakers: A Handbook of Worship Resources*, Buxhall, Suffolk: Kevin Mayhew Ltd.

Ian Bunting (ed.), 1993, *Closer to God: Practical help on your spiritual journey*, London: Scripture Union.

Heather Child and Dorothy Colles, 1971, *Christian Symbols Ancient and Modern: A Hand-book for Students*, London: G. Bell & Sons.

Gerald Coates, 1994, *Walk With Me: Meditations on the Way of the Cross*, Great Wakering, Essex: McCrimmons.

Esther De Waal, 1992, *Every Earthly Blessing: Celebrating a Spirituality of Creation*, Ann Arbor, Michigan: Servant Publications.

Doris Jean Dyke, 1991, *Crucified Woman*, Toronto: United Church Publishing House.

Virgil Elizondo (ed.), 1992, *Way of the Cross: The Passion of Christ in the Americas*, Maryknoll: Orbis Books.

John Finney, 1996, *Recovering the Past: Celtic and Roman Mission*, London: Darton, Longman and Todd.

Jim Forest, 1997 (expanded edition 2008), *Praying with Icons*, Maryknoll: Orbis Books.

Bede Griffiths, 1992, *The New Creation in Christ: Meditation and Community*, London: Darton, Longman and Todd.

Richard Harries, 2005, *Art and the Beauty of God*, London: Continuum.

Crispin Hollis, 2000, *Stations of the Cross*, Chawton, Hampshire: Redemptorist Publications.

Kenneth Leech, 1994, *We Preach Christ Crucified*, London: Darton, Longman and Todd.

Sara Maitland, 2009, *Stations of the Cross*, London: Continuum.

Thomas Merton, 1971, *Contemplative in a World of Action*, New York: Doubleday.

Janet Morley (ed.), 1992, *Bread of Tomorrow: Praying with the world's poor*, London: SPCK for Christian Aid.

Jaroslav Pelikan, 1987, *Jesus Through the Centuries: His Place in the History of Culture*, New York: Harper and Row.

Sue Pickering, 2006, *Creative Ideas for Quiet Days: Resources and liturgies for retreats and days of reflection*, London: Canterbury Press.

Sheila Pritchard, 2003, *The Lost Art of Meditation: Deepening Your Prayer Life*, Bletchley, UK: Scripture Union.

Wendy Robins and Gillian Hawney (eds), 1992, *The Scandal of the Cross: Evangelism and Mission Today*, London: USPG.

Ian Tarrant and Sally Dakin, 2004, *Labyrinths and Prayer Stations*, Grove Books Worship Series 180, Cambridge: Grove Books Ltd.

Desmond Tutu, 1995, *An African Prayer Book*, London: Hodder and Stoughton.

Selection of Internet Sources

Ankh: http://en.wikipedia.org/wiki/Ankh; http://www.swagga.com/ankh.htm
Byzantine Cross: www.classic-crossandcrucifix.com/byzantine_crosses.htm
Celtic Cross: http://www.seiyaku.com/customs/crosses/celtic.html; http://wikipedia.org/wiki/celtic_cross
Coventry Cross of Nails: http://www.crossofnails.org/about/; http://en.wikipedia.org/wiki/Coventry_Cathedral
Crucifix: http://en.wikipedia.org/wiki/Crucifix; http://www.classic-crossandcrucifix.com/crucifixes.htm
Early Christian Symbols: http://www.jesuswalk.com/christian-symbols/cross.htm
Good Friday: http://www.newadvent.org/cathen/06643a.htm; http://www.woodlands-junior.kent.sch.uk/customs/easter/goodfriday.htm
Greek Cross: http://www.seiyaku.com/customs/crosses/greek.html
Holding Crosses: www.hadeel.org; www.thechristianshop.co.uk; www.eden.co.uk; www.scotiafairtrade.com; www.holdingcross.com/
Irish Crosses: http://www.sacred-texts.com/pag/idr/idr29.htm; http://www.crosscrucifix.com/articlehome.htm
Jerusalem Cross: http://seiyaku.com/customs/crosses/jerusalem.html
Labyrinths and Prayer Stations: www.yfc.co.uk/labyrinth; www.labyrinth.org.uk; www.freshworship.org; http://jonnybaker.blogs.com
Latin Cross: http://seiyaku.com/customs/crosses/latin.html
Making the Sign of the Cross: http://en.wikipedia.org/wiki/Sign_of_the_Cross; http://www.fisheaters.com/sign.html (and many more)

Maltese Cross: http://www.2.prestel.co.uk/church.oosj/cross.htm
Prayer Stations: http://jonnybaker.blogs.com
Religious Crosses: http://www.siyaku.com/customs/crosses/index.html;
   http://crosses.org/history.htm
Russian/Eastern Orthodox Cross:
   http://www.muhlenberg.edu/depts/forlang/LLC/rus_cult/Toolweb/papers_2.htm
Stations of the Cross: http://en.wikipedia.org/wiki/Stations_of_the_Cross;
   http://www.stjohncathedral.co.uk/prayers/stations/index.htm
St Andrew: http://www.seiyaku.com/customs/crosses/andrew.html
St Brigid: http://www.crosscrucifix.com/articlehome.htm
St Cuthbert: http://seiyaku.com/customs/crosses/cuthbert.html;
   http://wikipedia.org/wiki/St._Cuthbert
St Dominic and the Dominican Order: http://en.wikipedia.org/wiki/St_Dominic;
   http://www.tntt.org/vni/tlieu/saints/St0808.htm;
   http://www.seiyaku.com/customs/crosses/dominican.html;
   http://en.wikipedia.org/wiki/Dominican_Order
St Francis: http://www.franciscanfriarstor.com/stfrancis/stf_san_damiano_cross.htm;
   http://www.shrinesf.org/francis10.htm;
   http://sfoskd.tripod.com/id41.html
St George: http://en.wikipedia.org/wiki/St_George's_Cross;
   http://www.baronage.co.uk/2002c/stgeorge.html
St James (Cross): http://en.wikipedia.org/wiki/Cross_of_St_James
St James (the Way): http://en.wikipedia.org/wiki/Way_of_St_James
St Thomas: http://en.wikipedia.org/wiki/Rock_crosses_of_Kerala
Sun Cross: http://www.seiyaku.com/customs/crosses/sun.html
Swastika: http://wikipedia.org/wiki/Swastika
UK National Retreat Association: info@retreat.org.uk. For Christian hospitality
   across Europe see http://www.christian-hotel.com

Pictures of Crosses

Peter E. Ball, 1999, *Icons of the Invisible God*, Newark: Chevron Books. For a list
   of commissions in church buildings: www.petereugeneball.com.
Benedictine Nuns of Turvey Abbey, 2000, *Stations of the Cross* (set of A4 pictures),
   Great Wakering, Essex: McCrimmons.
Gabriele Finaldi et al., 2000, *The Image of Christ: Seeing Salvation* exhibition
   catalogue, National Gallery, London, New Haven: Yale University Press.
Julia Hasting, 2000, *Crucifixion*, London: Phaidon Press Ltd.

Janet Hodgson, 2006, *The Faith We See: Working with Images of Christ*, Peterborough: Inspire, Methodist Publishing House, with CD-ROM.

Images of Christ: Religious Iconography in Twentieth Century British Art, 1993, London: exhibition in St Matthew's Church, Northampton, and St Paul's Cathedral, London.

Images of Salvation: The story of the Bible through medieval art, 2004, CD-ROM: Christianity and Culture, St John's College, Nottingham.

Ron O'Grady, 2001, *Christ For All People: Celebrating a World of Christian Art*, Geneva: WCC Publications.

Stations: The new sacred art, 2000, Bury St Edmunds Art Gallery.

St Paul's Audio Visual Productions, n.d. *Man of the Cross, The Passion of Christ Today*, Set of 15 Posters based on a modern artist's interpretation.

Masao Takenaka, 1975, *Christian Art in Asia*, Kyoto: Kyo Bun Kwan with Christian Conference of Asia.

Masao Takenaka and Ron O'Grady, 1991, *The Bible Through Asian Eyes*, Auckland: Pace Publishing with Asian Christian Art Association.

USPG, USPG Church of Ireland, CMS, Methodist Church, 2000 (2nd ed.), *The Christ We Share* Resource Pack, London: Methodist Publishing House.

Hans-Ruedi Weber, 1979, *On a Friday Noon: Meditations Under the Cross*, London: SPCK with Geneva and Grand Rapids: WCC Publications and Wm Eerdmans.

Roger Wollen, 2004, *The Methodist Church Collection of Modern Christian Art: An Introduction*, Peterborough: Methodist Publishing House

Hymns Relating to the Cross

Abide with me – Henry Francis Lyte (1793–1847)
All you that pass by – Charles Wesley (1707–88)
And can it be – Charles Wesley (1707–88)
Broken for me, broken for you – Janet Lunt (1978)
Christ the Lord is risen today – Charles Wesley (1707–88)
Come and see, come and see – Graham Kendrick (1989)
Crown him with many crowns – Matthew Bridges (1800–94)
Freely, for the love He bears us – Timothy Dudley-Smith
From Heaven You came, helpless babe – Graham Kendrick (1983)
He gave His life in selfless love – Christopher Porteous (1959)
In the cross of Christ I glory – John Bowring (1792–1872)
Jesus is Lord! Creation's voice proclaims it – David Mansell (1979)

Lift high the cross – G. W. Kitchen (1827–1912) and M. R. Newbolt (1874–1956)

Lifted high on your cross – Pulling Bracken

O sacred head, sore wounded – attrib. to Bernard of Clairvaux, Paul Gerhardt (1607–76)

On a hill far away stood an old rugged cross – George Bennard (1873–1958)

Rock of ages, cleft for me – A. M. Toplady (1740–78)

Saviour of the world – Greg Leavers (1986)

See Him on the cross of shame – Ruth Hooke (1987)

Take up thy cross, the Saviour said – William Gardiner (1770–1853); Charles Everest (1814–77)

Thank You for the cross – Graham Kendrick (1985)

The head that once was crowned with thorns – Thomas Kelly (1769–1855)

There is a green hill far away – Cecil Frances Alexander (1818–95)

Were you there when they crucified my Lord? – American Folk Hymn

What kind of love is this – Bryn and Sally Haworth (1983)

When I survey the wondrous cross – Isaac Watts (1674–1748)